GAIA

Our Precious Planet

DEDICATION

I dedicate this book to both Mother Earth,
our precious planet, who gives to all the families
who live upon her so much abundance, and to my own
family from whom I have learned so much.
I love you all. I truly hope that through
the words of this book families may
unite and form loving bonds of
understanding and compassion
for each other. This is the
way love will spread.

The Earth was small, light blue
and so touchingly alone;
our home that must be defended
like a holy relic.

- Soviet cosmonaut, Alexei Leonov.

Also by Barbara McDougall:
Tara, Emissary of Light
A Crack in the Cosmic Window

GAIA

Our Precious Planet

A Galactic Perspective
of Human Evolution

Barbara McDougall

The Oracle Press

PUBLISHED BY THE ORACLE PRESS
P.O. BOX 121 MONTVILLE QLD 4560 AUSTRALIA

National Library of Australia

ISBN 1 876494 01 8

Printed by Watson and Ferguson & Co., Moorooka, Qld. 4105

ACKNOWLEDGMENTS

I wish to acknowledge all my students who have given me so much encouragement for the work that I do. I value your support so much. My heartfelt thanks to my husband and partner in life, Bruce, for your love, stability.and belief in me. Your earthy practicality brings balance into my life.

My appreciation to Brian Priest from The Oracle Press for his calm and balanced evaluations and for the professional way in which he puts my books together. He makes the publication of them seem so easy. I also would like to express my thanks to Graham Wheatley of Watson, Ferguson & Co. who printed this and my other books, *Tara, Emissary of Light* and *A Crack in the Cosmic Window*.

Ibi Pusztai has once again come to my aid to proofread this story for me and my thanks go to her for her dedicated approach. Ibi was so engrossed with this story when she read it for the first time that she wasn't able to engage her Virgo brain into analysing and discriminating any incongruities in the writing. She had to finish it first and then go back to do the detailed work of inserting commas, correcting paragraphs, spelling etc. I am so grateful for her professional approach and it is such a pleasure for me to work with her.

Melody, American author of the wonderful *Love is in the Earth* series, lovingly offered to write write both the foreword and the back cover endorsement for *Gaia* and I thank her deeply. Her support for both *Tara, Emissary of Light* and *Gaia, Our Precious Planet* have touched me deeply. She is a very special being of light.

Most importantly I wish to express my deepest thanks and love to my cosmic guides who transmit messages to me, especially the Arcturians, who transmitted this story.

I give my loving gratitude and thanks to Gaia, our precious planet. My heart feels so full whenever I look around and see the abundance of natural beauty that you provide to all living things. It is my heartfelt desire that, through the words of this story, many others upon the planet may also feel deeply into their hearts and souls and learn to appreciate your gifts of love.

Finally, and with deep humility, I acknowledge and give love and thanks to our Prime Creator, the Divine force behind our existence. It is such a great privilege to be a part of your wondrous creation.

CONTENTS

FOREWORD BY MELODY

I am genuinely honoured to be writing this foreword to *Gaia - Our Precious Planet*. Barbara is a kindred spirit to all of us and her light work in bringing together both healing of the Earth and cohesiveness in society is a working, paramount example for all of us. During my reading of her manuscript I found that I was enthralled and compelled to keep reading. I just could not put the book down!

Barbara shows, through *Gaia - Our Precious Planet*, a new look at evolutionary development and how we can all facilitate living in harmony with all of nature by being conscious of our own personal connection to the creative source of all that is.

The messages within the pages not only address the problems of today but provide solutions we can all implement. They reveal such universal truths as: experience of individuality is primary in experiencing a joyful evolutionary path; whatever one creates will be one's total reponsibility (from inception to completion); trusting in one's own intuitive processes will provide the correct path for change, acceptance of personal responsibility for one's own thoughts, emotions, and energy required for advancement; and that expansion and cultivation of our consciousness, our light and understanding, can assist in healing ourselves and our world.

She provides prime examples of how our thoughts are energy and can affect both harmony within the self and harmony within humanity, and shows how we can cease in giving away our power through fear-based emotions, and both begin and continue to facilitate our utilisation of our energies at their highest and best.

Barbara validates, through *Gaia - Our Precious Planet* that the time for choice is NOW, that the choice is yours alone, and that you, individually and collectively, can assuredly make a difference. Unified harmony with our Earth has always been of prime importance in my life. My books are all dedicated to the Earth, and I have experienced the loving care that many have taken in the care of our Earth. I know many of the light workers who are living now on our Earth and are continually sending heartfelt love and healing to our Earth; many others, including mineral miners I know, are, in addition, assisting with the renewal, restoration and replanting.

You, the reader, will find yourself sending thoughts and feelings of love and healing to our Earth as you read this book, and forever after; you will find that your thoughts and feelings are both received and acknowledged with love returning from our 'jewel of the galaxy', our Gaia.

- Melody, author of *Love is in the Earth*.

INTRODUCTION

The main body of this book came through me with the greatest of ease during a four-week period in January 1998. The first part of the book was transmitted to me some months previously.

It is my regular practice to meditate most mornings, even if only for a few minutes, as I find this calms and centres me, which in turn keeps my body functioning in a healthy state.

For the past few years I have been transmitting focussed light and love energy to Planet Earth, and specific troubled spots upon her, during my devotional practices. I do this as I believe it assists in clearing dark energy that create imbalances upon her. Towards the end of these practices I often receive messages which I write down with my non-dominant hand, my left hand. I endeavour not to engage my left brain, that rational, logical, critical side, as I do not want to influence the messages in any way. I simply write down that which I hear

Gaia, the story, had a powerful impact on me. As the story unfolded I could feel, and see, all that was occurring. Visual pictures were created in my mind through the words that were coming through. My senses and emotions were activated as each day's writing unfolded.

My husband was also profoundly impacted by the

story as I read it to him. He felt it deeply. It opened up new doors of perception for him. My husband was also profoundly impacted by the story as I read it to him. He felt it deeply. It opened up new doors of perception for him and answered many questions such as: why the races on Earth are different in skin colour and culture; how we as humans have evolved to the level of consciousness that we experience today; how the many power brokers can covertly as well as overtly, influence our lives for their own selfish ends if we allow it, and most importantly, what we as individuals can do to help bring peace and harmony to our own lives and to life on Earth.

It is my deepest hope that this story will strike a cord in your hearts and will open you to understanding more about yourself and the way your energy impacts others, as well as Gaia. It is my greatest desire that you will be able to objectively and lovingly change consciously any self-destructive thoughts and behavioural patterns you play out in your life so that you too can begin to live in a state of internal peace and harmony. This way you will not only be aiding yourself, your family and friends, but also aiding Gaia, this precious planet we call our home. God bless.

- Barbara

Part One

1. THE FIRST CIVILISATION

A very long time ago, when the Earth was young, the beings upon her lived a very peaceful, fulfilled and contented life. All their needs were met. They had natural shelter, plenty of food and the sun warmed their bodies. Temperatures were even. There was no great distortion or range of extremes in temperatures. That happened much later.

Human beings lived in harmony with all of nature. All were considered equal. All had their place in the great scheme of things. All were respected for the roles they played.

Trees and plants were honoured as valuable members of society. Birds and insects were honoured and valued for their contribution. Animals were honoured as were the creatures of the sea. Mother Nature was pleased. Earth was honoured and gratitude expressed daily for the bounty she provided. All lived in harmony with the Divine Plan.

The Prime Creator was pleased with the way its creation was manifesting. All was created in its same likeness – that is, all with a spark of divine energy. Each species, human, plant, animal, insect, fish – all were created from the same stuff – the energy of the Divine Creative Source.

The Divine Creator then had an idea – an idea that

would bring about change. The Divine Creator understood that, though living in absolute harmony and peace was blissful, there was very little growth or evolution when perpetually in this state. All was of a group consciousness and there was no awareness of individuality.

The Divine Creator desired to expand – to grow and experience more. This meant that if the Creator was to do this then all parts would also expand, grow and experience as all was connected to that Divine Source. This idea pleased the Divine Creator and so this thought form was sent out to the ethers. A change was about to occur, a change to the existing status quo.

The Prime Creative Source didn't know what the humans on Earth would choose to do with this energy of change. They had free will to choose their path for themselves. They were free to make this change easily, through love, or they could choose to make their changes through difficult experiences. Each one would need to make this choice personally.

All the Prime Creative Force knew for certain was that change would occur and the change would result in expansion, growth and conscious understanding, and that evolution of the species would occur as a result. In time, human beings would become more conscious of themselves as individuals and become conscious of their own personal connection to the Creative Source.

The Prime Creator waited.

Humans were slow to pick up on the Creator's idea. They were used to instinctual, habitual living and their ways were quite fixed. They didn't want to change. They liked being in their comfort zone. They liked operating the same way as they had always done. It felt safe and secure. They refused to change and evolve.

Then, centuries later a strange and unusual sight appeared. What seemed to be strange flying objects littered the sky. There were many of these objects that looked like massive birds, hovering over the people. The people were not afraid, as they were not used to that emotion, however, they were curious. They watched and waited.

Ladders of light seemed to appear from the belly of the flying things and human-like people descended. They were tall, masterful and were obviously more highly evolved than the humans on Earth. They raised their hands in peaceful gestures and the people encircled them wanting to touch these unusual visitors from the sky.

The visitors communicated telepathically to the inhabitants, advising them that they had come to Earth specifically to teach humans new ways and to assist with their evolution. They told how they had felt impulsed to come through promptings from the Divine Creator. They said the reason for life on Earth, and on other planets and star systems, was for all living things to evolve, through experiencing, to a higher conscious under-standing of themselves and their place in the Universe and as all life evolved and expanded in consciousness, so too did the Creative Source.

The space visitors said it was time for earthlings to become more conscious beings through experiencing a greater variety of emotions, feelings and thoughts. As humans had demonstrated their unwillingness to make this change for themselves then an outside influence was needed in order for this evolutionary leap to occur.

"The time has come," the visitors said, "to begin a new phase of your evolutionary journey. You have been stuck in your old patterns of thought and behaviour for too long. You have become static and dull. We are here to assist and serve you. We are here to teach you new ways of thinking and being. We come in loving service. We are willing to teach you our ways of living, our understanding of natural law. You only need to ask us."

The inhabitants of Earth listened to the words of the visitors. They felt unusual feelings stirring inside their bodies that they had never experienced before. The visitors were certainly bringing change. It could be felt by all. Some felt their hearts beating, some felt queasiness in their stomachs, some felt excitement like electrical currents running through them. They all experienced something different. They began to experience individuality.

The Prime Creator smiled. The idea was beginning to be made manifest. The Creator wondered what humans would do with these new feelings and experiences. Would they create for themselves an easy, joyful evolutionary path, or would they create a path of sadness, negativity, lack and darkness? Whatever they created would be of their own doing.

As time went by the space visitors intermingled with humans. They lovingly taught them many things. They introduced new ways to help them select and prepare food. They showed them healing plants. They taught them about the energy from their solar system and how to work with it for the best results.

These space visitors kept to their own kind. They did not inter breed with the humans on Earth. They simply wanted to pass on information of a practical nature to help aid human development. The visitors enjoyed their holiday on planet Earth. It was such a beautiful place. They called it the jewel of the galaxy, as it seemed to sparkle with such radiance and beauty at all times.

Mother Earth was pleased with the visitors' love and care and grew even more beautiful. Her lakes and seas shimmered with light. Her forests grew taller and greener, her plants and flowers grew more profusely. Greater abundance was created. Much laughter, love and joy were felt by the masses. Harmony prevailed.

Eventually these space visitors left Earth. They had served the humans on Earth well. They had taught them much and the inhabitants of Earth had been eager students. All benefited from the interchange. The beings on Earth had evolved greatly, becoming more individualistic.

Then many, many aeons after the space visitors left, some humans became lazy. They felt it took too much effort to live in accordance with the ways of the space visitors. They began to rebel and opt out of the community programmes that the visitors had introduced. They didn't want to do their bit for the community. They wanted to do for themselves only. Selfishness was being experienced quite strongly by many people. A new, destructive energy entered the consciousness of some humans.

These individual thought forms collected together to form a mass. Over time this mass grew bigger as more and more individuals became more and more selfish. This mass of dark thought form energy impregnated itself into the minds of other humans. The destructive energy spread. Some humans who felt this impulse had the mind control to understand where the thought was coming from and were able to direct it back to its source with love but most were unconscious and unaware.

As time passed, it became apparent that more and more humans were buying into the negative, dark thought forms. More and more people rebelled against the communal ways. People became dissatisfied with their lives and became envious of the freedom they perceived others experienced and they wanted to experience the same thing. Mother Earth felt this unrest. She wasn't feeling so balanced any more. Parts of her began to feel dis-eased. She was picking up on the darker energy currents that were being experienced by the humans.

Millenia passed. Humans, as a mass, now lived unfulfilled lives. They did not experience the peace and joy of living. Their lives became empty and devoid of meaning. They became more and more robotic in their day to day activities. They lost contact with their hearts, their connection to the Earth and their feelings of love.

Mother Earth tried to awaken them by displays of assertiveness. In order to shake off the negativity that was all over her, created by humans' thought forms, she birthed volcanic eruptions. She shuddered and shook in her pain and agony and released her emotions through earthquakes. She cried huge tears and there were tidal waves. Still humans didn't get her message. They didn't understand that their negativity was energy and that energy was creating disease and disharmony within Earth. Human living worsened. People did despicable things to each other. They murdered, butchered, raped and denigrated each other and the land that nourished them. Often they ate each other and even sacrificed young children to appease their 'gods'. They lost all connection to the divine spark of energy that was in their hearts.

A black period descended on Earth. There was very little light in the hearts and minds of the people. Obsessed with power, destruction, lust, envy and greed they had no time to devote to their children, their families or their community. Their only focus was on selfish pursuits – how they could get what others had – how they could take whatever they wanted. A whole value system based on getting, rather than giving, developed.

Mother Earth had had enough. She wasn't valued by the people anymore. She was defiled, abused, disregarded and desecrated. Enough was enough. She collected all her internal energies, her will, and with intent, exhaled deeply. Her waters rose and spilled up all over the populated lands. Where there was once land there was now water. She belched and land rose up where there used to be water.

An entire civilisation of humans was wiped out. There was no human alive to tell the tale.

Mother Earth calmed herself and her boiling emotions subsided. Her entire surface was transformed, never to be the same again. She prepared herself for a long period of rest and recuperation for she knew she needed to heal her wounds. The sun's energy would warm her and give her light. She rested, peacefully.

Part Two

1. SECOND PHASE OF EVOLUTIONARY DEVELOPMENT

We the Arcturians greet the people on Earth with love and warmth. We choose to assist humanity with their evolution to a higher frequency. We do this at this specific time in Earth's history as a means of preventing even greater calamities.

We have been monitoring humans' progress on Earth over many millennia and recognise the time has come to offer assistance. People on Earth are at great risk of destroying their precious planet. This is something that we of the Galactic Federation cannot allow. All people need to learn to live in peace and harmony on planet Earth. Other star systems, more highly evolved, do not engage in warfare or destruction as they have moved on from childish games.

We, the Arcturians, offer our services to you and we ask that you consider our words and take them seriously. One way we can be of assistance is to relate Earth's history to you in a way that can be understood by many. We are here to tell a story, a true story that will touch all those who read it.

The story starts millions of years ago when Gaia (Mother Earth) was young. She was created according to the Divine Plan to be a haven of rest and recuperation for visitors from far distant galaxies and star systems, to be a haven of beauty, a place of abundance. She was created to be a home away from home. Beings from other galaxies visited her frequently and rejoiced in her beauty and abundance. They passed on their experiences to others.

After millennia, some beings who were experiencing difficulty living on their home planets and star systems decided to make Earth their home. They could see that she had much to offer. They purposefully left their own well-established way of life to begin living a primitive yet abundant life on planet Earth.

They often re-visited their old home bases in order to bring back to Earth specific aids to assist their lives. As Earth time went by many other beings from different systems in the galaxy also chose to leave their planet of birth and reside on planet Earth. These beings formed colonies in different parts of the planet, each unaware of the others existence.

The colonies established were self sufficient and well organised. Life was good and harmony prevailed. Both male and female lived as equals. There was no hierarchal system – the greater good of the whole was always the prime motivating force for any decision making. As more and more beings came to live upon Earth, the colonies expanded.

There were three distinct colonies – one colony had beings with a predominantly dark skin colour, one had beings with a reddish colour to their skin and the other colony had beings with a more yellow tone to their skin.

Much time passed and many Earthborns now lived in the colonies. Many of these Earthborns had no experience of any other home. They only knew Earth. They often heard their families speak about 'home' and their origins from the stars and this developed in the Earthborns a quest for adventure. They wanted to explore their home, planet Earth. As more and more of these young beings grew to maturity the desire to explore their home planet strengthened. They formed exploration groups and began moving beyond their own home territory. They planned their journeys well and took many provisions as they anticipated being away from home for some time.

It was inevitable that at sometime in Earth's history there would be a meeting of all those communities that lived upon Earth at that time. At first these meetings were friendly – all species were amazed to find others living on the same planet. There was much interaction and communication. They were at different levels of evolution yet all had evolved beyond confrontations and wars. Even though their systems were different they all understood Universal Law. They lived according to the dictates of nature. They lived in harmony with the land, never taking more than that which was needed for survival and always replacing whatever was taken with something of equal value. The customs of the three main species living on Earth were totally different and so each group learned much from the others. They found pleasure in inter-mingling and learning about the others' way of life.

Peace still reigned on Earth. Gaia was happy.

Millions of years passed. All living things prospered on Earth. A state of balance existed. Visitors still came from other galaxies, however, they could not always be seen by the natives as the visitors vibrated to a higher frequency. They emanated more light and love than did the humans. Many of the beings living on Earth had given up their spiritual practices, focusing totally on physical pursuits. They also had begun indulging in selfish, destructive thoughts and emotions, thereby lowering their vibrational level and creating dense energy in their energy fields. The dark, dense energy emanating from them gathered mass and in time created a dense aura around Gaia. This denseness of energy made it more difficult for the local inhabitants to see the space visitors.

This situation applies today.

2. THE BEGINNING OF DESCENT INTO DARKNESS

It was a calm, quiet and peaceful morning when all of nature seemed to glow like crystal dew drops when a dark, large and quite ominous space ship appeared in the skies over one of the settlements on Earth. This spaceship was huge – as big as a large city. It seemed heavy and dense yet hovered quietly as if made from air. This was the time in Earth's history when the descent into darkness began.

The space ship was occupied by beings from a far distant region who were under the power of a being with a very dark consciousness. Some call this consciousness the Lucifer consciousness. This being, or consciousness, wanted control and power over others. He wanted to take from others for his own selfish ends.

He had been viewing planet Earth for some time and began to covet its unique resources. He had watched how races had flourished. He could see the wealth that was inside Earth in the form of crystals and minerals. As Gaia's energy field changed and gathered dark masses it attracted him. He felt it was time to make his move. He knew there would be humans upon Earth who could play a power game with him. When the light was bright he had not been able to make his move as he needed the darkness in the form of negative thoughts and emotions in order to act.

The community on Earth that were the first to experience the Luciferic impact were not at first concerned when they viewed the black ship above them. Unfamiliar with the emotion of fear they lived in harmony and balance with nature and so had developed and rapport and trust for all that nature provided.

The dark ship hovered for a whole day and night before anything else occurred. The community were in darkness as the ship cast such a giant shadow. Then, on the second day a group of beings dressed in black robes, each with an enormous headdress shaped somewhat like a bird, lowered themselves onto a platform under the ship. They communicated in a dictatorial, authoritarian and commanding manner stating that they had come from a far distant galaxy and were on a mission to aid their own planet. They told of their great weapons and then physically demonstrated their weapons' power by targeting an area just beyond the community, reducing it to nothingness within an instant.

The Earth community then felt fear – it rose from the collective as a dark stream of energy. It could be smelt.

As the invaders could read energy they knew they had made a lasting impression on the earthly residents. The invaders also knew how to manipulate the minds of others for they understood how the consciousness that is within every living thing is connected to the Creative Source as an energy stream and that all beings are part of the whole. These dark beings knew how to manipulate energy by manipulating the consciousness or minds of being. They were masters at this game. Their aim was to get this community to work for them; to be their servants and slaves, whether the beings did this consciously or unconsciously didn't matter – so long as it was done.

The beings of darkness knew that the emotions of fear and powerlessness generated weakness in consciousness and they fed off these emotions. The energy of fear en masse created wonderful food for the invaders as it enabled them to feel more powerful and energised.

The community on Earth had only a vague understanding of this universal principal and were in such an open and trusting state that they were vulnerable to the influence of the Luciferic consciousness. They became the slaves and servants of the dark beings, becoming pawns in a hierarchal system. Their lives changed. No longer did they feel peace and harmony inside of them. No longer did they live loving and productive lives. The emotions of fear and powerlessness played havoc with their consciousness and their physical bodies.

After aeons of time the invaders decided to move on to the next community on Earth, using the same tactics of control and power. They left behind in the first community many overlords who ruled the community through fear. They were quick to annihilate any who revolted against their command. The dark beings from a far distant galaxy devoured the light consciousness of other communities on Earth and created instead a mass of consciousness that was both fear and powerless based. This dark energy from both the invaders and the inhabitants permeated the energy field of planet Earth. Planet Earth, as a living organism, also has a consciousness. She was created by the Prime Creative Source to be a Garden of Eden – a place of beauty and balance, a place of tranquillity and peace, a place of abundance. Her role in the great scheme of things was now being threatened as a blanket of darkness enveloped her. Her energy field was polluted by the dark energies emanating from the species that now lived upon her.

This dark energy made her feel unwell. It didn't feel comfortable to her. It was a shock to her system. She allowed the darkness to continue for many millennia hoping that there would be some beings on her that would understand what was happening and take appropriate action. However, her auric field was becoming so black from all the dark energy around and upon her that she realised action needed to be taken. She knew she was the only one who could do anything about the situation. She knew she needed to be responsible for her own auric field.

An agreement had been made at the time of her creation to always be a haven of beauty for all who came to visit and all who lived upon her. This agreement was now in jeopardy through no fault of her own. She recognised it was up to her to bring herself into alignment again knowing also that if her darkness increased then that energy would flow out into the solar system and affect other planets in her realm of influence. This she could not allow.

Mother Earth heaved great sighs of sadness and great chasms opened in her belly causing simultaneous earthquakes and tidal waves. The seas heaved and were in turmoil as Gaia's hurt was expelled from her being. Then she began to feel rage welling up. "How dare these beings living on me desecrate me – how dare they dig inside my body and extract my energy storage system for their own good! How dare they use my body for their own ends!"

The consciousness of Earth contains darkness as well as light as does all living things, however, it is when the balance is tipped in favour of darkness that imbalance and disharmony occur. Gaia recognised the disharmony within her energy field and she chose to release her darkness because she had the greatest good of the whole as her concern.

Cataclysmic earth changes took place. The whole land structure changed. Mostly all the inhabitants on Earth perished. Some of the dark beings escaped the destruction but most suffered the fate of the masses.

Gaia rested – at peace again. Harmony had been restored. However, the souls of all those that had perished now contained the memories in their consciousness of the fear, the powerlessness and the catastrophic events. Some souls contained the memories of the power-hungry games they had played. Each individual soul had their cells imprinted with their own relevant information. They would carry these memories with them into their next, and subsequent incarnations, and these memories would form part of their conscious way of living. Karma had been created.

So it was and so it is.

3. THE REBUILDING OF THE HUMAN RACE

A few beings, surviving the cataclysmic events that occurred on Earth at that time, eventually formed the human race as we know it today. They managed to survive through their instinctive and intuitive behaviour as they were the ones that were in tune with nature and the animal kingdom. They had lived on the outskirts of society and hadn't become caught up in the control games that were perpetrated at the time. These beings had been counsel unto themselves, and had felt the animals' discomfort and had also experienced changes inside their bodies, as if they could feel Gaia's pain. They were sensitive to, and aware of, their own bodily messages. They had acted on their own body's information and intuitively knew huge changes were to take place and had trusted their own intuitive processes. Though their survival seemed miraculous evolution must take place and Mother Nature ensured that it did. These surviving species became more animalistic in their nature and learned to survive through instinct rather than logic thought. Over time their numbers increased, however, for aeons they remained small groups scattered around the globe.

Gaia provided abundance again – fruits and vegetables grew, sustaining the inhabitants. As these beings relied on their instincts for survival their mental abilities diminished. Their thought patterns became slower and their brain atrophied.

Earth again was viewed by beings from other galaxies and star systems to be a haven of rest and recuperation – a playground of beauty. Many visitors enjoyed her abundance and observed the devolution of the species with interest. The natives were unable to see the visitors because they had devolved to such a low frequency level.

At the appropriate time in Earth's evolutionary history a decision was made by the Galactic Federation (the overseers of many galaxies) to seed the earthlings with extraterrestrial knowledge and wisdom in order for the evolution of the species to accelerate.

It was also time for Gaia to begin her evolution to a higher frequency and therefore an opportunity was created for the humans upon her to evolve with her. Gaia was conscious of this timing and had, in fact, asked for assistance.

The Galactic Federation asked for volunteers to aid this work. It was explained to the volunteers that their commitment could involve multitudinous lifetimes on Earth as their genes would mix with the Earth species and they would suffer a great density of vibration as the beings on Earth had devolved to such a low frequency. It was also explained that the volunteers would be aiding the Prime Creator's plan if they chose to commit to the task.

Many beings from other star systems and galaxies volunteered for this service to the Divine Plan and so a strategy was devised that would take many, many millions of Earth years to fulfil as it needed to be taken at a pace that could be integrated by the earthlings.

Galactic time is quite different to Earth time so the volunteers had no concern for that aspect of their mission. They were motivated by their desire to help creation on Earth evolve and they were willing to experience this evolution as their service to the greater good. The plan was put into action and many beings from other galaxies and star systems descended into Earth's energy field.

Earthlings were unable to see the visitors because their earthly frequency levels were so low. Their 'radio band' of thought only worked on one particular frequency range and they were not able to tune into a higher frequency. Their eyes could therefore only see that which their minds could understand.

The first role of the galactic volunteers was to aid the earthlings via thoughtforms – to imprint ideas that would penetrate their denseness. This would enable earthlings' lives to become more productive and effective. This took a great deal of patience and love. However, gradually, the earthlings became less animalistic in their approach to life and began to think – albeit in a limited way.

At the same time as this was happening the galactic volunteers introduced many different animal species to Earth. They also brought many grains and seeds, introducing these different species as an experimental study. Many of these species of animal and plant thrived in the pleasant conditions on Earth and so Gaia became even more abundant.

The next part of the plan involved the volunteers actually living on Earth and forming colonies – as had happened so long ago. They chose to lower their own frequencies so that earthlings could see them, as their intention was to inter-breed in order to raise the genetic level of the species.

Again this took millions of years of Earth time. However, it was accomplished and very highly evolved communities formed. Not only were the galactic volunteers living on Earth and inter-breeding but also many other beings from other galaxies and star systems chose to live on planet Earth and enjoy her abundance and wealth.

Some of the volunteers chose to work with particular tribes who lived in very fertile areas. This particular group of visitors had a great empathy for the land and had a deep understanding and love of nature, having chosen to work and live predominantly using their intuitive mind. They formed communities of self-sufficient groups who allowed their heart and spirit to guide them in their daily activities. These visitors taught the local inhabitants how to increase their intuitive and psychic abilities, how to tune into the energies of the plant and animal kingdoms and how to maintain balance and harmony with nature.

This civilisation is called Lemuria or Mu by some on Earth. Its landmass was huge, occupying much of your present Pacific Ocean. Many of your indigenous races now living around this area originated from this civilisation. The ancient people were taught to honour and respect the land, not to take from her more than that was needed for their own survival, and to always give back to the land whatever they could to redress any imbalance.

Other inter-galactic volunteers and free settlers were more interested in left brain development. They were interested in architecture, science and mathematics. Their focus was on building cities of splendour and beauty and also advancing scientific studies and experiments. This civilisation is called Atlantis by some humans today. It existed in much of your Atlantic Ocean.

Both civilisations were advanced beyond the species on Earth today. Both civilisations were large and successful. These two civilisations extended over a large area of the Earth's surface.

For a long time they prospered, each in their own way. Millions of years had now passed since the time those few earthlings survived the first great cataclysm. These earthlings were now genetically blended with beings from other star systems. They were now coded in their energy fields with a different, more highly evolved, energy system. They understood the principals of reincarnation and understood how universal law worked. Understanding and respecting their energetic connection to the Divine Source they practiced spiritual rituals and devotions regularly. These highly evolved species on Earth at this time were well aware of the principle of energetic balance and understood that each individual needed to be responsible for their own energy so they were able to use the abundant natural energy that is always in existence for their own sources of power, individually and collectively.

In the civilisation, called Atlantis by some, the use of crystal energy was very prevalent. This energy was harnessed by the Atlanteans and the volunteer galactic representatives also utilised it to aid the progress of the species on Earth. It was used by many for healing purposes as is happening on Earth today. It was also used as a transmitter and receiver of higher frequency energies from other dimensions.

At this time in Gaia's history she was able to bask in her love energy. Even though there were beings upon her that were being prompted and controlled by the Luciferic consciousness the greater mass of thoughtform energy emanating upon her from the population was of a higher and lighter vibration – a loving vibration. Most beings respected and valued her and worked and lived according to natural laws. They did not abuse her or show her contempt. They did use her crystals for their own source of power, however, they were always careful to dig the crystals from those places upon her energy grid system where there would be the least damage.

Many pyramids were built over high energy vortices to amplify Gaia's grid system. They used these pyramids as temples for their contact with other space beings. The crystals that were in the temples were programmed to be receivers of sound waves.

There was a specific design to the building of these pyramids as they formed precise mathematical and geometric formations, inter- connect-ing through streams of energy. These inter-connected temples helped to keep Gaia's energy field balanced and harmonised. This technology is only now becoming available to humans today. It was well understood and utilised at the time related by this story.

The Luciferic consciousness, which represents the

dark or negative aspect of consciousness – which is needed for evolution – was at this time in our story working in a covert manner, mainly using thought control as a medium of expression. When any beings living on Earth allowed themselves to feel fear, jealousy, resentment, revenge or any other dark emotions, or chose to sacrifice their own energy – their power source to another – or when they took another's energy through domination and control, the Luciferic consciousness knew these beings were ripe for thought penetration. Luciferic consciousness feeds off negativity. It is their fuel. The covert forces of darkness were at work playing their underhanded games.

The architecture in the cities of Atlantis was magnificent and the knowledge these beings had of space, light and mathematics enabled these buildings to serve many purposes. Some acted as healing centres, designed in such a way to utilise the energy from the cosmos to its highest and best. Simply standing inside the buildings created healing. The cosmic energies of sound and light were understood and utilised for the greater good of all.

The human species, now interbred with the galactic visitors, had raised their cellular level to a much higher vibratory rate. They were not so dense in physical appearance and their brain capacity had increased greatly. Their heads were shaped more conically to that of humans today, and their pineal and pituatory glands were more highly developed. They were able to 'tune into' higher frequencies and dimensions with ease.

Many were still unable to grasp the concepts of the more highly evolved souls, however, all had come a long way through the interbreeding of the volunteer galactic beings of light.

Aeons of time passed and many people became complacent. Some gave up their spiritual rituals through laziness. Many gave up attending the sacred temples and healing centres. Many allowed their psychic and intuitive abilities to atrophy as they allowed their own energy fields to become lower in vibration. They allowed thoughts of negativity to enter their consciousness and were too lazy to continue being personally responsible for their own thoughts, emotions and energy.

This was what the Luciferic consciousness was waiting for – a space or a vacuum that they could fill with negative thought programs. They were hungry. They wanted power and control. They wanted fuel.

As they imprinted some of the less aware and conscious beings on Earth with their dark thoughtforms, these thoughtforms quickly gathered mass. Thought is energy and as such moves very quickly. When there are enough thoughts of similar kind the energy groups together and forms a mass. This mass can become an entity in its own right – with a very dark consciousness. And so it was.

When enough dark mass was formed over Gaia it was observed by some dark power and control-hungry beings from other dimensions. They smelt it, felt it, saw it and knew it was time to act. They were magnetised to the energy under the Universal principle of 'like attracts like'. They went in for the 'kill'. They gathered masses of their crafts and their weapons in order to take up station above Earth.

Some of the inhabitants of Earth could sense and see these dark beings with their inner vision and warned the leaders of the land. However, the leaders were complacent, enjoying their status and power and chose to ignore the warnings.

The dark beings decided to infiltrate through stealth rather than by overt means. They accessed the minds of those weaker and less responsible beings, those that had less awareness and understanding of energy, and bombarded their minds with thoughts of power, envy, jealousy and greed.

The dark aliens wanted their own puppets in positions of power and control over the masses. Once this was achieved they would use the energy of fear to control them for their own ends. They also planted thoughts of genetic engineering methods into their puppets' minds knowing that through the manipulation of the DNA of the earth species they could gain power and control over the masses as well.

Working with implants of an energetic nature they were able to implant a 'box' of energy into a puppet and could then trigger this implant whenever they chose – over countless incarnations – until such time as the puppet became aware and was able to consciously seek aid to remove it. This was a wonderful way of triggering negative dark emotions in people as a source of food for the dark aliens. It provided them with an endless supply.

Once the now manipulated puppets on Earth began coveting power for themselves and their own selfish ends, the energy field around Gaia changed. The mass of dark energy became greater than the mass of light and love energy. Gaia felt it. Her consciousness was affected. She began to feel ill from the polluted thoughtforms of those living upon her.

She, as a responsible consciousness, couldn't allow this to continue. She remembered her past. She decided that this time she would give warnings to the people who lived upon her. She would create earth tremors and mild volcanic eruptions in the hope that the people on Earth would become aware of their own destructive games and take action.

Some people did understand her warnings, especially those that had a great affinity with the land. They listened to their bodies, watched the animals and observed Gaia. They took heed and prepared themselves. Most people did not, especially those in powerful positions. By now their egos were well and truly under the influence of the Luciferic consciousness. Having no thought for the greater good of the whole they had no empathy with Gaia, or with their underlings. They simply wanted power and control for themselves.

They wanted to be recognised by others as powerful people. Seeking fame, they liked the feeling their power over others gave them for they liked to feel more important than the masses. They chose to close their hearts to love and to perpetrate negativity and darkness instead. Many began to have heart problems but chose not to look to self for cause.

Some of these people were high-ranking scientists and managers involved with the crystal power technology and genetic engineering experiments. They managed to attract to them people of like mind who were also into power, greed and control. These people were under the influence of the Luciferic consciousness but were unconscious of the process.

They were so obsessed with the idea of power that they wanted to create the most powerful container of power that had ever been built. They built crystals of immense size and energetic capacity, bigger and larger than anything that had ever been attempted before. For this they enlisted the aid of all the best minds and did not advise them of their true purpose but told them instead that this tremendous power station was needed by the growing population. They fed their assistants lies. The project was huge and was carried out in secrecy, again another trait of darkness. At the same time the genetic engineers were working on stripping humans and mixed breeds of their 12-stranded DNA. They did this purposefully so that they could produce a race of robots, people whose conscious understanding of themselves and their place in the Universe would be diminished greatly. They wanted a team of robots working for them, not teams of highly evolved, free thinking people with advanced, inquiring minds.

Both projects were successful. Human evolution took a very backward step at this time. The balance between light and dark was being destroyed once again in favour of darkness. The genetic engineering teams created an army of clones – robot like humans. They also did experiments with mixing animal and human genetics producing a distorted species. Many drawings of these species exist in your records today.

The advanced beings in this culture still travelled

intergalactically. Their spacecraft took them to other planets and star systems and to other places on Earth. They had tremendous freedom and those in power utilised their space travel fully.

Gaia was becoming restless. Her warnings had not been heeded by the masses. Her energy levels were falling again. Her belly rumbled with excess pollution. Again her agreement was in jeopardy and again she needed to act to clear all the darkness and dense energy from her field. She issued another warning – this time far more extreme. She created huge tidal waves that engulfed the shores of the lands upon her. There were more earth-quakes, much stronger in intensity than previously, and more volcanic eruptions.

Those in tune with her knew it was time to leave the area – it was time to find another home, either on Earth or on another planet or star system. They made their preparations and departed. They were few in number.

Those involved with the giant crystal project were nearing the time when the experiment was to be tested. The dark space beings watched and waited. They were pleased with their efforts. They were pleased with their puppets. They felt powerful and filled with energy and had great fun triggering their puppets' implants. They laughed at the results of the genetic engineering experiments. All was going according to their plan.

The day arrived for the testing of the giant crystal. All was in readiness. When the charge was activated, not only did enormous energy surge out the top of the crystal into the cosmos, blasting everything in its path, but the energy also charged down deep into Mother Earth's belly with such force that it split the land asunder. Great chasms formed instantly – buildings crumbled – seas erupted.

Gaia was jolted, shocked, pierced horribly. Her waters boiled, chasms deepened – cities crumbled. The atmosphere was split with enormous charges of energy. Lightning flashed, storms raged, darkness reigned. Tumultuous seas engulfed the land. Atlantis fell into the cavernous realms of the deep. All who were on the continent perished. An enormous part of Earth's land was lost beneath the sea. Lemuria's land mass totally changed and most perished. Earth's advanced civilisations ended.

The seas subsided, storms abated and Gaia began to heal. Over time her energy field became cleansed once more of negative thoughtforms. Her body, however, still smarted from the sudden and violent piercing of her internal structure. She rested. Her experiences were forever imprinted into her memory banks.

The souls of those who died in that cataclysmic event also contain memories of that time. Those that escaped through using their psychic and intuitive abilities have their memories and those that perished through abuse of power and ignorance also have their memories. These memories can be accessed now by any who choose to do so. The lifetimes spent in Lemuria and Atlantis are imprinted on the soul memory of all people on Earth.

People living on Earth now are replaying some of the roles they played then, albeit unconsciously.

As it was, so it is.

4. THE GALACTIC MISSION

Sometime after the demise of Atlantis and Lemuria, a group of volunteer beings from another dimension of time and space were given an exciting mission to perform. A challenge had been given to them by the Galactic Council. They had been chosen for this mission from a great number of volunteers because of their own special unique qualities and their ability to work as an integrated and loving team.

The group chosen, we shall call them X, were both excited and a little overwhelmed at the magnitude of their task. However, as they felt greatly honoured to be selected and were committed wholeheartedly to their mission. They intended to complete it successfully. Their mission involved accessing the records that were stored in the energy field of a particular planet in one of the far distant solar systems. What an adventure lay ahead for them. Never before had any of the team travelled so far from their own sector in space. They were to be away for as long as it took them to complete their mission success-fully. Preparations were made and all became ready for departure. They were farewelled by the Galactic Council and were given their instructions.

These beings were highly evolved and had no need of space vehicles or weapons. They were filled with light and their hearts filled with love. The energy that vibrated within them was of a very high frequency. They were almost transparent because of the quality of light that emanated from them. Their highly tuned consciousness enabled them to manifest themselves in whatever frequency range they chose, simply through focussed thought.

As a group they focussed on the specific planet called Terra, or Gaia, and within a split second of earthly time found themselves in that dense energy field. The X Team chose to manifest themselves at a place in Earth's Northern Hemisphere. The area was isolated – barren and bleak. The X Team surveyed the scene. It was uninviting and felt sad to them. This place had suffered some form of severe deprivation. There was very little life around. It was cold and much of the northern continent mass was covered in ice. This ice appeared to be melting as if some impactive event had caused the breaking up of the ice mass.

The team tuned into the records, the memories contained within Earth's energy field, and the pictures began to form. They saw the beauty and splendour of Gaia's creation, they saw the love and attention shown to her. They saw her as a jewel in the galaxy. They also saw the pictures of destruction and felt such compassion and empathy for her plight. As they poured their love into Gaia's field, they knew she would feel it and respond. They saw that Gaia was weary and had experienced a terrible ordeal that had left her weak and vulnerable. Team X could not have arrived at a better time. They agreed to spend some time on Earth and offered to aid Gaia in her recovery process.

Tuning into her they felt her greatest need was that of peace and harmony. Her body had been split asunder in her recent past and she had not yet recovered fully, even though thousands of earth years had passed since the great calamity had befallen her. She was still feeling pain in her belly, often acutely. She needed love and positive thoughtforms around her.

Team X decided to travel around Earth's surface investigating, gathering information for their records and at the same time aiding Gaia by sending their thoughts and heartfelt feelings of love.

The team practiced group rituals each morning and evening at sunrise and sunset. At this time of the day, when the energies were high, they were able to tune into the higher realms and make contact with the Galactic Council. They telepathically passed on their findings thus far and advised the Council of their plans.

Deciding on their first area of focus they all agreed they needed to objectively view Earth from a distance in order to see, or feel, where the greatest negativity upon her was situated. Once this was established they could then teleport themselves to that place and then work on creating harmony and balance. Focussing well they could see many small places of light upon Earth, obviously where humans were living in small groups, living according to natural law and thinking mainly positive and uplifting thoughts. This was pleasing and Team X decided to visit these places at a later time.

However, they also saw a very dark heavy cloud of dense energy in an area of land beside a large river. This was the area they chose to visit first. As they transported themselves to this place they felt the denseness of energy penetrate their bodies. It took an enormous amount of effort and will to cleanse themselves of this darkness. They could also smell fear.

The presence of some pyramids indicated that at some time in the past these people had been evolved and knew how to use and understand universal energy. They wondered what had happened to cause the denseness of etheric energy. Making their way to the pyramids they observed the beings that lived in the area. There seemed to be a lot of building going on and masses of people were scurrying hither and thither like a myriad of ants. All were anxious and fearful. These people seemed human but were in fact slaves.

The team was astonished at this behaviour. They had never witnessed anything like this before. They felt compassion for the mass of people who were being persecuted.

Team X tuned into the energy field of the area searching for some light amongst the darkness. When they found the light they made their way to that place. It was a temple, not unlike the buildings they had on their own planet. They felt joy, as they knew there were others who could aid them on their mission. There were many females inside the temple, calm, serene, loving and open. These women greeted the team without fear, extending warmth and love. A small group of older women told the team their story, verbally handed down to them by their family. Their forebears had left Atlantis at the first signs of Gaia's pain and had come to this place. They had been drawn to Egypt because of the pyramids that were situated on energy vortices and as such were places of contact with beings from other realms. Their forebears felt at home in these surroundings.

At first they had intermingled with the local inhabitants and there was peace and harmony in the land. They had built their temples and many people came there to be healed. They performed spiritual rituals and adhered to natural law. Life was good. However, as time passed many of their highly developed skills began to diminish. Some time ago, beings from the most distant planet in the solar system landed in the area. They were huge in stature and their craft was dark and quite enormous. They called themselves gods and expected to be treated as superior. Their mission was to take from Mother Earth specific minerals that were lacking on their planet, in particular gold. They needed this precious metal and knew that Earth had great quantities.

These gods were not really evil. They just wanted what they needed to aid their own planet and their own people. These gods were of a family called Anu and they were from a planet some on Earth now call Nibiru. Two sons were allocated extensive areas of Earth to rule and to mine for gold. The gods didn't like doing the labour themselves – this wasn't part of their plan – so they needed to have others do it for them.

Most of the population of this area was not, in the eyes of the gods, highly evolved. They created their own clones – beings that could carry out menial tasks for them. These were the slaves the X Team saw prior to visiting the temple.

The temple priestesses were silent at the conclusion

of their narrative. Feeling great sadness they could see that the team was feeling this way as well. The priestesses said they had tried to reason with the Anu but had little success. All they could do was to keep the temple pure and clean of negative energy, practice spiritual rituals, heal those who came to visit and stay in integrity and love themselves.

The team decided to visit the gods themselves and found them to be quite charming and open. The gods enjoyed parties and having a good time. They showed no interest in the team. They were a little curious but that was all. The Anu were enjoying their sojourn on Earth and expected to achieve their objectives. Once this was done they would return to their home planet. They only had opportunities to visit Earth infrequently because of their home planets' large orbit around the sun; 3600 years according to Earth time, and so they intended to avail themselves of their current opportunity.

They listened when the team explained the plight of Gaia and momentarily were moved to feel slight sympathy but it was only fleeting. Their own agenda was far more important to them. The gods suffered no pangs of guilt when the team explained how their greedy mining practices destroyed Gaia's energy grid system and invaded her belly, causing her pain. The Anu invited Team X to come again to another party and politely but firmly asked them to mind their own business.

On returning to the temple the team made the decision to move on as soon as they had shared some new teaching methods to the temple society. Sharing some of their own rituals with the priestesses they showed them how to send thoughts and feelings of light and love to Gaia in the sure knowledge that it would be received and acknowledged.

Team X also formulated some new loving thought-forms, which became pods of light energy helping to dissipate the dark. They set up classes teaching natural law and how to live lives of quality, love and truth and encouraged the local people to visit the temple, especially the children, The priestesses agreed to continue all the teachings.

Meanwhile, the gods were still enjoying themselves, manipulating the clones and any other earthlings who allowed themselves to be manipulated. They loved counting all their gold. Having built huge structures for their crafts and beautiful homes for themselves, they then encouraged their clones and any other earthlings to worship them by creating images in their likeness. They enjoyed the feeling of power this gave them.

The beings from Nibiru have a more metallic structure to that of humans and do not have your feeling capacity. This changed a little when they experienced sexual intercourse with humans. Often the daughter, Inanna, enjoyed sexual interaction with the earthlings. She found this stimulating and fun and experienced feelings she had never felt before. She found she really felt love for some of her human male earthlings. Her brothers enjoyed their sexual intercourse with the human females as well. There were offspring from these unions, half god and half human, who carried a more highly evolved genetic structure than did the other earthlings and so were revered by the locals.

You have many records of these times in your history and many more will be discovered.

Team X moved on. They had done all they could. They had dissipated some of the dark energy over the area and had left many teachings for those who chose to learn. They would have liked to have done more but they knew they couldn't interfere with humans' lives as this was against Galactic law. They respected each individual's right to exercise their own free will and knew that karma would accumulate for them if they interfered with this law.

The team could see the Anu were creating much karma that would have to be repaid at some time. The gods would eventually draw to them states of powerlessness and would find that state difficult to handle. However, that was their business.

Moving on to the next area that needed balancing, Team X once again viewed Earth's energy field from afar and saw another great mass of darkness. They wondered what thoughts and emotions emanating from the people had caused this imbalance. They found they needed to be acutely aware of their own individual energy fields as the third dimensional energy was much denser and heavier than that of their own planet and it would have been easy for them to absorb that denseness.

They transported themselves to an area north of Egypt between two large rivers where the influence of the gods was still highly prevalent. People in this land had built temples to worship the gods and had constructed many icons and sculptures in the gods' image. The natives revered and worshipped the gods and were in fear of them for they had seen them arrive in their space ships and believed they had come to rule them. Their fear was growing and that was the cause of the darkness in the etheric field of their land.

This race was highly creative and made beautiful pottery and mosaics. They had lived quite balanced, happy yet very primitive lives before the gods arrived. The gods of course fed them many stories, mostly as jokes, but the humans believed their stories and took them literally. Much of your history contains versions of these stories. The gods had taught the Sumerians how to build the temples by using some of the advanced tools they had brought with them. They also taught the Earthlings communication skills, including writing. The gods advanced the evolution of these people considerably. The people in this land of Sumer were impressed with the power of the tools and the power of the gods, and so they allowed themselves to fall into patterns of subservience, fear and powerlessness.

The team observed and recorded their findings and then sought to establish some means of dissipating the darkness without impinging upon the free will of the individuals. Again they sought light and again found priestesses in temples of healing. There were many such temples around this area so the team arranged for all the groups to meet and exchange views. Group rituals and meditations were practiced with the main focus being the raising of loving thoughtforms to counteract the negativity over the land. Team X encouraged the combined groups to start classes for children and teach them about energy, the power of thought, and how to live in accordance with nature's laws.

The time the team spent in Sumer was productive and successful. They knew, however, that their successes were only temporary. They were creating a breathing space for Gaia and this was all they could do under the terms of their mission. They were observers and recorders and as such needed to abide by their task.

Team X moved on to many of the less populated areas observing and recording the energy patterns created by the inhabitants.

Many pockets of humans were living very primitive lives, yet very much in tune with nature. They were able to communicate with the animal kingdom via telepathy and those groups who lived by the sea had learned to communicate with the dolphins through tuning into their frequency range. These facets of life was observed by the team and recorded. Sometimes, the team chose to manifest into the third dimensional frequency and make themselves visible to the various groups and sometimes they chose to observe and record from a higher frequency. They were enjoying their sojourn on Earth and found their experiences stimulating. They developed a great empathy and understanding for the earthlings and their level of consciousness. They realised the humans on earth had a long way to go before they would develop a higher level of frequency, a higher conscious understanding of themselves and their world. In fact, the team could sense and feel that humans would devolve even further.

Team X then visited many areas in the southern hemisphere where climatic conditions were more equitable and food was abundant. Most of the people practiced self-healing methods using plants and flowers as their tools. These people loved and valued nature and cherished Mother Earth. These indigenous races were those descendants of the Lemurian survivors. Most of these tribes lived in harmony with each other and with the land. They maintained a balance in nature, always choosing to act as a community for the greater good of the whole.

This then was the status quo on Earth around 5600 years ago. The population was dispersed around the globe with larger groups in more densely populated areas in the Northern Hemisphere. The cataclysmic events leading to the fall of Atlantis and the total destruction of that continent around 12,800 Earth years ago at the end of the Age of Leo had left an aftermath of relative calm.

Most groups of people in the inhabited regions were totally unaware of any other's existence. They lived their lives believing that their group was the only one on Earth. There was no means of travel and all the technology that the Atlanteans had developed had been submerged with the land. Memories of the advanced civilisations had been erased from human consciousness at that time and people became immersed in their own day to day survival.

Team X had done their work well. They felt their mission was successful. They had recorded an accurate account of the status of Earth and the people who lived upon her. They decided to visit again their original landing spot in the Northern Hemisphere prior to returning to their home and so again transported themselves to that place.

They tuned into Gaia once more and sensed she was

less weary. She had by this time greatly recovered from her past ordeal and was ready to begin the next phase of her evolutionary journey. Some dark clouds of negative energy were still around her but not to the extent they had been. Her belly had healed and she felt more stable and calm. Gaia expressed her gratitude for the work Team X had done in providing a breathing space for her. She said she was stronger and more able to diffuse the mass of negative energy around her – she could shake it off easily and not allow it to affect her. She felt in balance once more and so could send this balanced energy out to the other members of her family in the solar system. She explained to the team that when she was out of balance other planets in the system felt it also and this was why it was so important for her to guard her energy levels. She asked the team to thank the Galactic Council who had acted upon her request for aid by sending the team to her. She said she hoped she would never again need to ask for help.

The team fondly farewelled Gaia and performed a final meditational ritual, sending their combined light and love to the whole of Mother Earth and then focussing on the parts of her that showed darkness.

Focussing intently on their own home planet they felt waves of light engulf them. They quickly relocated into the higher dimensions, their denseness and heaviness washing away. They were elated with their endeavours and expressed their desire to the Galactic Council to return to Earth if ever there was to be a further mission.

And so it was.

5. EVOLUTIONARY CHANGES BEGIN

Gaia had now recuperated from her ordeal and again had many beings from other dimensions and frequencies visit, remarking on her abundance and beauty. The inhabitants on Earth were unable to see the visitors because their third dimensional energy field was now so dense.

Once the vibratory rate of a species is lowered and becomes slower through uncontrolled thoughtforms and emotions then the matter of their physical bodies becomes denser and their mind becomes closed to the reception of higher frequencies. When people, individually and collectively, become engulfed in their material world without a balance with the spiritual then they slow down their evolutionary process and their frequency level. Gaia's evolution to that of a being of higher frequency also slows when the energy of the mass of thoughtforms from the collective dulls her energy field.

However, she was content with her progress so far. She knew the time was not yet for her to evolve into star status. There was much more for her to experience before that event occurred.

Gaia again provided food, shelter and abundance for all living creatures upon her. She gave of herself freely and lovingly. As time passed populations around her globe increased and flourished. Mostly at this time men and women still lived in equality, each respecting the others' roles.

In some cultures on Earth at this time the female was regarded more highly than the male because she gave birth. She therefore was linked with Creation, the Source of all things. Females were revered and many ceremonies and rituals were practiced. The women were also revered because of their monthly menses and these times were considered sacred. The women would group together at these monthly occasions and go into retreat as they usually all menstruated at the same time. They allowed their blood to enter Mother Earth as they believed the energy contained in that blood would nourish Gaia. The women had discovered their menses period was linked with the energy of the moon and were aware of the ebb and flow of their blood tides each month. They were also aware of how the Moon's movements through the zodiacal signs determined their moods and feelings during each monthly cycle. The stars and planets in the heavens played a very big part in tribal life. People had much time to study the night sky to plot the effect of the celestial bodies on their lives. Wonderful stories were passed down through the ages and most people became knowledgeable about the energy from the stars.

Even though the female was venerated and respected she, as a collective, kept harmony within the groups. Some tribes of women did allow power to go to their heads and became authoritarian and dominating. These cultures soon found that the negative energy they directed out soon came back to put a stop to these behavioural patterns. Karma is always played out.

Mostly, at this time, the masses had little under-standing of the process of procreativity. People thought that the wonder of procreation was something that just happened. They had no understanding that the male provided the seed that was implanted into the female's womb from which the embryo would develop. When this concept was understood and the male recognised that he produced the seed that was responsible for the birth of a new infant, a change of status developed.

The males began to believe they were more important than the female. They had discovered a new sense of power. They thought they were the creators of all life. This new thoughtform gathered mass and moved like wildfire through the consciousness of humanity. A darker energy field began to develop as this thoughtform intensified. The thoughts and feelings of power, domination and control of the male species over the female grew and grew. The power the males felt seemed to make them more aggressive and demanding. It also led to rivalry, one believing he produced better seed than another. This also resulted in hierarchal traits. The ones with the better seeds were the ones that considered themselves rulers and leaders. This male supremecy developed strongly during the Age of Aries, some 4000 years ago.

Females began to be regarded as vessels, receptacles into which men could place their seed. Females allowed this to happen as a mass consciousness. They gave away their own power, their own sense of value. The thought-forms of the collective gradually became darker once again. Power, lust, control, possession and jealousy were now prevalent. Men fought more. There were more tribal wars as men wanted possession of land.

Women did their best to maintain their rituals and spiritual practices but the men became more and more controlling and demanding. Most women chose to play the subservient role although some rebelled against the male dominance. In the cities male dominance grew rapidly. Men took control of the communities, the state and religions. Men took over the temples and the priestess culture died.

Gaia could feel the changes upon her and could sense the time was approaching when she would lose her precarious balance again. She did her best to dissipate the negative energy by releasing her pain through earth tremors and volcanic eruptions. This helped keep her at ease.

The beings that visited her from afar observed the actions of the humans and wondered at their strange behaviour.

By now the original galactic volunteers had spent countless incarnations upon Earth, experiencing all that Gaia experienced. Often they spent lifetimes as healers or teachers of spiritual and Universal Law and often lifetimes in pain and violence. Their role was to experience all that was to be experienced on the third dimensional plane and then, when the time was appropriate for Gaia's ascension, to be there for her to aid her through her transition. They were the star seeds, consciousness that had chosen voluntarily to assist in the evolutionary process of Gaia. They usually forgot their mission as the dense atmosphere on Earth created amnesia and it was only in the spaces between incarnations that they remembered. It was at these times that they gathered their strength to carry on.

And so the stage was set for the next part of the evolutionary story.

6. THE DOWNWARD SPIRAL ESCALATES

By this time the Luciferic consciousness was gathering its forces. It had been gradually infiltrating the minds of humans and realised the time was ripe for a stronger penetration. As the male aggressiveness increased so too did the role of the Luciferic consciousness. This was the great opening it had been waiting for. Humans now allowed its deeper penetration. The more darkness humans thought and felt the more the Luciferic consciousness appeased its hunger. As the women allowed their subservient role to escalate and allowed the men to dominate and control them the more 'food' the darkness gleefully generated and devoured.

His-story was accelerating into a downward spiral.

The more power the men had the more they wanted. They became more and more greedy for control and domination. This also accelerated their sexual urges. As they felt their power over women increase their sexual urge became stronger. They loved to dominate. It felt good.

Equality of the sexes evaporated into the dim past.

Those spiritual beings from the higher realms were observing humankind fall into darkness once again and accepted the process as the free will choice of the humans. These spiritual beings adhered to galactic and Universal Law whereby one being could not interfere with the consciousness of another unless invited. They could only observe and record the progress of humans and also check on their volunteers' progress. They always made sure that, in the times of greatest darkness, there was incarnate upon Earth one of their more enlightened volunteers who could shed light into the darkness. Many such beings lived on Earth during these dark times. Krishna, Pythagorus, Plato, Socrates and Buddha to name a few.

The Galactic Federation knew that Gaia and the people living upon her needed to make their own choices as to whether they evolved or devolved. It was a personal choice and as such was respected by those from higher dimensions. Gaia had made her choice. It was her intention to evolve to a higher frequency, to become a star. However, she knew the celestial energy emanating from the cosmic bodies in the solar system and beyond needed to be in certain alignments before this could take place. There was still much for her to experience before that time arrived.

In the ancient lands of Sumer and Egypt there was now much activity. The arts and crafts and their writings, established by these people, spread to other areas. People travelled and different cultures intermingled. Some cultures believed in one God, one Creative Source of all things and believed the Sun carried the energy of this Creative Source. They worshipped the sun, giving it many names, including Ra.

Some cultures still worshipped a number of gods, creating idols and statues to remind them of their gods. Many clay tablets and artefacts now found have recorded the various belief systems of the different cultures on Earth at that time. Many such relics depict the gods from 'outer space'.

There was more and more blood shed in the name of religion as time went by. People fought over whose beliefs were right.

There were also wars fought over possession of land. Many war- like tribes of men invaded other civilisations simply because they sought power and land. Often the invaders would force their belief systems upon the local inhabitants.

Always, in some pockets around the globe, there were small groups of people who understood and practiced natural law. They understood how energy works and they lived by spiritual principles. They lived primitive lives by the standards of those in the civilised areas. However, they lived in harmony and peace with themselves and with the land.

The light upon Earth never totally went out.

Some forms of religion swept across the 'civilised' lands, mostly by force, as the invaders took over from the local people. They did not allow free will as that meant free thinking. They forcefully impressed their beliefs onto others. Believing their religion was the right one and any other was totally unacceptable. They generally thought their belief was coming from God. The worship of many gods was banned in most of the countries invaded and much hatred was perpetrated in the name of the one God.

Many religious books were written and filled with stories that were made up and embellished by power-hungry moguls, representatives of the church and of the state. They chose to write stories that would make the masses afraid and powerless. Often they created stories that depicted a punishing and dictatorial god. With the aid of the Luciferic consciousness these men in high places created a tool that would reach all civilisations on Earth through which the masses could be controlled. Some of the stories that were written did have a basis of truth in symbolic form. However, the power-hungry men made sure the messages were taken literally by the population.

Formalised religions were now prevalent and beliefs adhering to these religions were becoming stronger and stronger. People were expected to believe all that was fed to them without questioning. Those that questioned were dealt with severely, mostly by death.

The darkness increased. Gaia felt it deeply. She suffered. Some parts of her body were becoming polluted, not only with negative energy from dark thoughtforms but from the desecration of her natural resources. She would expunge her sickness when it became unbearable through the creation of earthquakes and volcanic eruptions and an occasional tidal wave.

The Galactic Federation observed – so too did beings from other star systems who had often visited planet Earth in the past. They were saddened by Gaia's plight but could understand, as they too had gone through that phase of evolution in their distant past. They prepared to assist however they could when they knew the time was right and when they were asked.

The gods who had made their home in Sumer and Egypt in earlier times also watched and observed from their place in space. They had been reprimanded by the Galactic Council for the part they had played in the devolution of the human species on Earth and were now rendered virtually powerless within their sphere of influence. Karma had to be played out. They experienced their own tunnel of darkness as they came to terms with the effects their power-grabbing behaviour had created. They had interfered with the free will of the inhabitants of Earth and were now receiving their just desserts.

Inanna especially felt remorse as she had truly loved the earthlings. She did her best to reconnect to the consciousness of the earthlings she had loved via mental telepathy and did often stir emotions of love in some of them.

The male grab for power, possession and domination accelerated even more. Human life, especially those believed by the hierarchy to be underlings, was considered valueless. People were killed indiscriminately whenever the so-called better people desired.

Some people chose to escape the tyranny and go into the non-civilised areas but these were few in number.

Fear grew and grew – like a mountain of darkness. The Luciferic consciousness had so much food now. It was elated. It already had many teams of humans working under its control – albeit unconsciously . So many seeds of darkness had been implanted, which were now fruiting with delicious ripeness. More and more seeds were springing up in the consciousness of humans that produced more ripe fruit. The darkness was now self-perpetuating. Those darker entities from other dimensions also enjoyed triggering their implants once again. They loved to see their puppets go into emotional and mental turmoil. This was good food and good entertainment.

Gaia shuddered, sensing the darkness closing in around her like a heavy wet blanket. Her strength was eroding. She didn't know whether she could shake off the wall of darkness around her again.

She made the decision to ask for help once more.

7. GAIA'S CALL FOR HELP

Gaia's call for help was heard throughout the galaxy. Her pain was felt by many. She was exercising her free will by asking for aid from the higher dimensions. This request is needed before any intervention can take place. When other beings from different planets and star systems interfere with another's evolutionary process without being asked to do so they are contravening Galactic Law and much karma awaits them. The law of cause and effect is an immutable universal law.

Assistance could now be given to Gaia and those consciousnesses upon her who also asked for help. Guidance from the higher realms is always readily available whenever the heartfelt request is made. Galactic council meetings were called and Gaia's plight was discussed. Many ideas were considered. Whatever plans were made needed to fit into the natural cosmic cycles as the solar system to which Gaia belonged is a fixed and mathematically calculable system. It has an order and structure to it.

The Council from the star system of Sirius offered to work with the order of the solar system, helping to maintain balance to all of Earth's cycles. They offered to work with the sacred geometry as they considered that to be their field of expertise. They offered to make sure that the planets within the system maintained their orbits. The Sirians also proposed to liaise with other beings in the galaxy to form a working committee of dedicated volunteers to bring messages of love and awareness to the sleeping inhabitants on Earth.

A suggestion to work on accessing the minds of those humans who were open and receptive to higher frequencies and who had asked for assistance for higher conscious understanding of themselves, was made so that that once the link was formed they could then offer messages and pass on information.

This offer was accepted by the Galactic Council as was the offer made by beings from the Pleiades.

The Pleiadians were feeling some remorse as they had been one of the groups who had gone to Earth earlier in her history and had planted their seeds into the species on Earth. They had not gone at Gaia's request as they had had their own agenda. They now realised they needed to right this breach of universal law and they were eager to pay off their karmic debt by doing all they could to assist humans on Earth. They offered to incarnate again and also to teach and pass on information via thought transmissions.

Their civilisation was thousands of years in advance to that of humans on Earth and they could see the catastrophic traps that humans were building for themselves, so they wanted to prevent great disasters from occurring. They offered to help humans to open their hearts to love, truth and wisdom, and to open to the realm of feeling. They offered to teach humans how to do this and also to teach them how to heal themselves of dark, deep emotional, mental and physical blockages that prevented the full expression of love.

At one particular time, when the Pleiadians lived on Earth, they created a calendar that depicted exact cosmic energies. They were experts at understanding the energy from the solar system and beyond and knew how the order worked. Their calendar was created to last for many thousands of years. This calendar, which is still used by people on Earth today, ends at the solstice in December 2012. The calendar aids humans on Earth to work with the cosmic energies, positively and accurately.

The Pleiadians knew that by this end time humans would have made their free will choices, consciously or unconsciously, as to whether they wished to evolve to a higher consciousness, e.g., a higher frequency, or to continue their involution and so remain stuck in their third dimensional energy.

The Mayan calandar could not continue beyond that time as that collective decision could not be known. The Mayans, from the planet Maya in the Pleiadian system, also knew that a band of higher vibrational light energy, known as photon energy, would be experienced by Gaia and all upon her towards the end of the 20th century, towards the end of the Piscean Age. This band of energy was the heralder of the new age, the Aquarian Age. This energy band of photon light would shake up the consciousness of humans and would assist with their awakening process. It would help humans access their ancient memory banks and bring to the light much subconscious knowledge of times past.

As both the Sirians and the Pleiadians vibrate at a much higher frequency to that of humans on Earth and are much more highly evolved in conscious awareness of themselves, they were in a position to offer their unconditional loving assistance. Though they are from different dimensions, they are united in their desire to aid Gaia and the humans living upon her.

Many other beings from different star systems and planets also volunteered their specific gifts and talents in service, including we, the Arcturians. We do our work in a similar way to that of the Pleiadians. We ask for permission to channel our messages of love and light through individuals whose frequencies are able to match those of our own. When we receive their permission we carry out our work. Sometimes the vehicle is unaware of our impulses and at other times the channel is fully aware. We consider it an honour to be able to serve humans in this way.

The Anu, from the planet in the outer reaches of the solar system, which some call Nibiru, also offered to heal the harm they had done so long ago. As their orbit travels by Sirius they offered to join with the Sirians in an alliance. The Anu were a little reluctant to offer their services as they were still smarting from their ostracism by Galactic representatives, however they were aware of the great damage that humans were doing to their planet and didn't want humans on Earth to blow Gaia apart. It was in their own interest to see her whole and healthy. They had their own agenda for joining the alliance.

The Galactic Federation knew that it was now time to re-activate their volunteers who had gone to Earth so long ago on their mission of service. The volunteers would need to complete their karmic debts, clear out any darkness still lingering and become the leaders of the movement towards light and love.

All this would take time, many, many centuries of Earth time, however the plan was set in motion.

The spiritual hierarchy, on their higher and finer frequency range, also volunteered to assist Gaia and the humans upon her and so the Galactic Federation formed a branch committee of representatives from all of these places. Their prime aim was to assist Gaia to move into a higher state of consciousness – a higher frequency band, and so enable her to evolve her status and fulfil her destiny. Her destiny effected so many other energetic beings in the galaxy and it was important her transition be as smooth as possible.

A highly evolved being offered to reincarnate upon Earth at zero time in order to bring the light and love vibration to humans on Earth. This being chose humble parents and his birth into Earth's field was recorded in the heavens. Many Magi or Astrologers knew a momentous event was to occur and prepared themselves well. This being was called Jeshua by some, Jesus by others.

8. THE BATTLE BETWEEN LIGHT AND DARK GATHERS FORCE

The dark forces were also gathering strength. They wanted to have more domination. They believed his could be achieved through manipulation and control of the masses by implanting more fear patterns.

Over many centuries of Earth time the teachings of Jesus were misconstrued to suit the whims of power hungry men. People were taught to fear a wrathful God and taught to fear the afterlife. This fear swept through the masses like a debilitating current. The Roman Catholic church became all-powerful and under its auspices much invasion and destruction was perpetuated. The Luciferic consciousness was enjoying its time of glory. Its teams of greedy moguls were working for it, some unconscious of the forces within them and some quite aware and conscious, choosing to work with the darkness.

The New World Order was at hand. People were manipulated to believe that they could place their lives into the hands of the church and state and that they would be looked after. As more and more people gave up their own personal responsibility for their lives, their health and their spiritual well-being, they became pawns or puppets to the Luciferic consciousness. People en masse allowed themselves to be manipulated through education. They were taught specific doctrines and told these were absolutely true. History was designed to suit the men who were writing it.

Some countries couldn't face the truth of their own actions so wrote the books from their own illusionary perspective. Each country, each group, had their own agenda.

At this time many secret societies began to flourish on Earth, mostly closed to women. These societies all had different levels within their structures. The lower levels were fed that which the upper levels deemed appropriate. The lower levels were indoctrinated to think a certain way and they couldn't rise to higher positions in the societies until it was proven they could be a pawn. These societies housed, and still house, the power brokers.

Populations increased. Countries became divided into rich and poor. Gaia had sufficient abundance for all, yet many people starved. Those beings, observing human nature from their higher perspective, were amazed at the inhumane actions perpetrated by those men in power. Races fought against each other, horrible and devastating violence erupted in many places on Earth. It seemed as if there was continual fighting right around the globe.

Greed became a religion and the pursuit of money became a primary goal in the hearts and minds of the masses.

Many more centuries passed and weapons that created horrible destruction were invented and used to kill others. Hatred, fear, jealousy, revenge, greed and power became the motivating forces behind human behavioural patterns.

Many new inventions were created that enabled

humans to lead sedentary lives. They became less physical in their day to day activities, choosing to shut themselves inside buildings all day long. They lost contact with nature. The material world was now all they knew.

Gaia suffered great imbalance. Her energy field became more and more dense and dark.

The power moguls plotted and planned their world domination, gleefully counting their possessions. They accumulated enormous wealth. They owned all the major financial institutions, all the weapon production and had their stooges in places of power within governments and churches. They manipulated food distribution and educational systems.

At the beginning of the 19th century, when modern science was still in its infancy, much progress had been made by the power moguls. They had planned the means whereby they could gain more power. They were careful with their plans – only those at the very top echelon of their New World Order knew what was being orchestrated. They had seen how important weapons would become so they purchased even more weapon-making companies and planted their own pawns in top management. They then orchestrated the First World War.

The power brokers had great fun selling their weapons to different countries that were at war with each other. Their puppets, like toy soldiers, were dying by the thousands but their new weapons were being tested. They were able to perfect their weapons through these experiential conflicts.

Engendering hatred between countries, they laughed at how easy it was to feed their puppets all sorts of false information. They made up stories and incidents and encouraged the masses to take sides. Once people are divided it is easy to incite violence. Their system worked well and they kept on refining it. They didn't want any hiccups down the line.

Their net grew larger and larger. They encouraged people to procreate because the more people the more toy soldiers for them to play with and manipulate. Many new inventions were made during and after the First World War. It was a wonderful field for fertile progress. Of course, there was also propaganda to write – the puppets needed some reason for the war and they needed to be fed some information that would sustain them.

The power brokers had great fun manipulating the world depression and the stock exchange collapses following the war. The growing importance of money encouraged them to purchase major banks as well as large food distribution outlets.

Science became a respected subject and people in most civilised countries now believed that if you couldn't see or touch something then it wasn't real.

The First World War was so successful for the power moguls that they quickly planned another. They had accumulated so much wealth and had placed themselves in even more powerful positions in governments and financial institutions.

They planned and plotted how to take over the minds and bodies of the masses. Having captured mostly all the minds of the civilised world, the mass consciousness by now couldn't think for them-selves. The people were so indoctrinated to believe all that they read and were taught by the establishment that they were easy pawns.

Next on the agenda was to bring them into sub-servience through their bodies. Health was a potentially huge industry.

The Luciferic consciousness kept on implanting seeds of negativity and doubt into the minds of humans and fed off their fear and shame. Its puppets, the power-hungry brokers, stimulated the masses into negative thoughts and actions. Humans forgot they had free will. They forgot how to be responsible for their own thoughts and their own energy. They forgot how to find peace in nature. They forgot how to feel balanced and harmonious inside themselves. They forgot how to love.

There were still small pockets of light in some areas on Earth. Wherever people still lived in harmony with nature, expressing gratitude to the Divine Creator for all their abundance, and still lived according to their traditional ways, there was peace. Their inner life reflected their outer life. These people valued, respected and loved Mother Earth and were grateful for her abundance. They shared all they had with other members of their tribes as had always been their custom. They had not been exposed to 'civilised' concepts so they lived their lives in harmony and balance.

The Second World War was a great plan. It would be bigger and better than the first. Much technology would result and, of course, so much more power, control and money would be generated. The power moguls could hardly wait to get the game started. They had been watching a particularly dark young man for some time who had been encouraged to learn about the use of etheric energy – how it worked and especially how to manipulate it consciously. He had been well trained in dark occult law and was looking forward to putting his knowledge into practice. His mind was carefully impregnated with dark and manipulative ideas and he quickly learned how to use these ideas to his advantage. He loved the surge of powerful feelings he had when engaging and manipulating thousands of peoples' minds. As he received his energetic buzz, so too did the Luciferic consciousness. It fed off his energy. The more people he could manipulate through his words, the more he and the dark forces felt a high.

His hatreds and prejudices ruled him. His darkness overtook him. He followed the dark and chose to ignore the light that was within him. His armies were numbed to the reality of the situation and followed his direction blindly. They gave up their personal responsibility and became as sheep. They too, ignored their own internal light.

The Second World War again surpassed the expectations of the New World Order. Not only had they discovered the most potent weapon ever invented in modern times but they had divided the population into winners and losers. They now had a new propaganda to play with. They also had a lot fewer clever money handlers to battle. They amassed even greater fortunes and moved into even greater positions of power. Wonderful technology resulted from the war and great progress was made in the scientific field, especially with weaponry.

During the earlier part of that war there was some interaction with intergalactic beings which led to many scientific advances. These extra terrestrials had their own agenda and wanted to experiment with human bodies because their own race was dying out. They needed some specific genetic material from humans that would enable their species to survive.

They made deals with various governments but didn't honour their agreements. They did give out selected information and they did abduct many human and animal species and experiment on them, as per their agreement, however, they did so with far greater numbers than had been agreed upon. The governments sold out their people for advanced information because they wanted more power. The governments were powerless to stop the surge of abductions and so felt, momentarily, a sense of betrayal. However, the governments, powerless to stop the process, used their intricate systems to cover up this minor hiccup and continued to keep the information secret.

The weapons that were developed, partially through experiments and partially via the ET knowledge, were now so powerful they could blow up large areas of Earth. This was sensitive terrain. Not even the New World Order wanted that. The power brokers wanted to have masses of people to control not have them perish through violent nuclear destruction. They had to come up with other plans.

They had been having success with their drug, prostitution and gambling rackets so they decided to focus on these areas. They knew that the more people became addicted to these pastimes the weaker they became and therefore the easier they were to manipulate.

A whole new game was opening up. They placed their team members in leading positions in these industries and watched and waited. More and more money came rolling in to them and consequently more and more power. The more addicted people became, the more money they needed to feed their addiction and the weaker they became. A whole new army of puppets was being created.

People en masse began to forget their earlier religious indoctrination and embraced their new saviours, their addictions, with great fervour.

Gaia was rebellious. Her energy field was dark, her belly smarting from all the nuclear testing. Her energy systems were disturbed as her precious metals, her energetic anchoring points, were being ravaged. She felt she was being raped day after day. There were only a few people who really cared for her now. The masses were so involved in their material lives that they gave no thought to her. She felt neglected, abused, ravaged and betrayed. She couldn't understand why humans were so uncaring and disrespectful to her.

She needed to release her feelings in order to feel calm inside, so the number of earthquakes grew, as did the volcanic eruptions. The turbulent weather patterns reflected the turbulence inside humans. There was now famine and drought in many areas due to the pollution in the atmosphere caused by the pollution inside humans' psyches. Gaia was getting restless. Her time for ascension was approaching. She tried to maintain inner harmony but it was difficult for her. Humans were creating so much darkness, so much greed and so much hate and were abusing her resources excessively. Her anger was growing along with her restlessness. How much more could she take? She tried to tune into those areas of light that were still upon her and this eased her pain a little. She knew it wasn't yet time for the masses to awaken to higher conscious understanding of themselves and their world and wondered whether she could hold out until that time.

She knew the beings from the higher dimensions were putting their plans into place and this nurtured her.

Meanwhile the men in high places had been working steadily towards their goal of total world domination and control of the masses. They were now insidiously penetrating the major medical organisations all around the world and had planted their stooges in positions of power. Of course, most of the individuals had no idea that they were being manipulated through mind control programmes. They also became the puppets for the New World Order. As a mass they closed their minds to well proven ancient healing techniques and focused on new 'modern' medicine. They were taught it was better to drug people and cut them up rather than seek the cause of the illness and seek to prevent illness occurring. The drug companies rubbed their hands with glee. The more their drugs were used, the more money they made and the more power they had. They encouraged the medical organisations to remain closed minded and to become cohesive systems, supporting their own members wherever they could, irrespective of personal ethics and values, often to the detriment of their patients outside the system.

In some civilised countries modern medical and drug

organisations banned traditional healing methods, encouraging the masses to believe that the new methods were far more advanced and superior to the old, even though the new methods had only been trialed for 80 years or so and ancient traditional healing methods had been trialed for thousands of years. Their propaganda was most effective. People believed it and so aided and abetted the power brokers because they didn't want to take personal responsibility for their own health or their own bodies. They wanted some outside force to fix them up, so gave away their power to others.

Of course, the Luciferic consciousness loved this. It gobbled up the negative energy emanating from those who chose to play powerless, savouring every morsel. The power brokers could see their plan was working as more and more people were becoming totally dependent on the 'experts' for the functioning of their lives. The masses believed all that was fed to them via the media, they believed all that the medical fraternity extolled, they believed what their churches taught and they believed what their politicians sprouted. The masses were so gullible. They gave their power away to the dark forces.

They had lost the ability to see the big picture of their lives and had given up their ability to think and question for themselves as individuals.

What a wonderful opportunity for the dark forces to grow and grow. The power moguls rubbed their hands with glee. They could see their plan for total control and the formation of a one-world government was taking shape very quickly. They wondered how they could introduce more fear into the mass consciousness, knowing that fear of any kind renders people powerless. Fear was a wonderful weapon for them to use to get their own way. They also felt it was time to cull some of the population as Earth was getting a bit crowded. They tossed around various scenarios and decided to give germ warfare a trial. They were now against nuclear war as they themselves might get blown up and that certainly wasn't on their agenda!

Some of their puppets were happily playing with many species of germs and mixing up all sorts of interesting concoctions. Some concoctions were proving to be quite potent. Viruses were tested and one particularly strong one was selected to be let loose on a native race, just to trial it for research purposes! The virus worked in a horribly debilitating way and many became ill and very weak. The disease spread to many other countries. People started dying. A new horror was sweeping the planet, something to be feared greatly. As the disease ravaged more people, more fear was generated. A monster had been created – a monster that would go on to devour millions.

People were becoming more powerless. The plan perpetrated by the power-hungry men was well advanced. Stooges placed in high places in governments were encouraged to make the people dependent on them. The more people became dependent on the government to fix their problems for them, the more control the governments had over the people. Governments promised safety and protection from all problems. They encouraged people's dependence on their systems by handing out money magnanimously. The people, of course, were so grateful they voted them back into power. It was a good plan to create more control to the power brokers. The power brokers continued with their games – having fun and manipulating all the players.

Most areas of life were now managed and controlled by the dark forces. They had purposefully infiltrated the minds of humans and were succeeding with their plan beyond their wildest expectations.

The media and most communication networks all over the world were now under their control. They had strong guidelines as to what could be published and they encouraged as much violence, hatred, destruction and fear to be released as was possible as this would engender more weakness in the masses. It would also make the masses more accepting of all kinds of darkness. It was an insidious way to change the value systems of the masses. Money and greed were the basis of the stories released. More money was paid for stories of darkness. Money was the god.

Human values had now changed. People valued material goods, possessions and status above all else. The mass consciousness of people on Earth had become dark, dense and very, very heavy. More and more violence and crime were being committed as more and more people allowed their dark natures to rule them.

People wanted more – more sex, more drugs, more money, more possessions and would do whatever they could to feed their desires.

The forces of darkness were content.

9. THE LIGHT EMERGES

It was time for Team X to be called again. The Galactic Federation could see they needed the team to again go to planet Earth to observe and record exactly what was taking place in that sector of the galaxy. Team X were asked if they wanted to serve the Divine Plan once more and they eagerly agreed. They knew how important it was for Gaia to ascend to a higher frequency of light and love at the appropriate cosmic time as so many other energetic bodies in the galaxies depended upon it. They willingly and lovingly agreed to enter Earth's atmosphere and do what they could to assist Gaia's plight.

Preparations were made and advice was given. They were told that the Earth's atmosphere was much heavier and more dense than the last time they visited due to the excess pollution from both man-made conscious abuse as well as etheric heaviness. They were told of the great imbalance that existed between light and dark and how the dark now weighed more heavily than the light. They were warned they would be in danger of becoming caught up in the dense energy and that it would take effort and focus to remain centred and balanced.

Team X spent their preparation time raising their energy levels to higher frequencies through focussed spiritual practices. They wanted to be in as strong a vibration as they could achieve before they made their descent to the third dimensional frequency. They did experience a rocky ride, far more difficult to that of their previous visit. They elected to enter the Earth's gravitational field at a specifically auspicious time according to the positions of the planets moving through the zodiac in the solar system. They were trained in cosmic science, the study of astronomy and astrology, and understood that the energies emanating from the different cosmic bodies affected Gaia and the mass of humans upon her in differing ways.

They chose to enter Earth's gravitational field at the spring Equinox in the Northern Hemisphere because day and night were equally balanced at that time. The symbolism of this equinoctical period was appropriate, as part of their mission was to help Gaia become more balanced.

They were amazed at the population explosion that had occurred since their last visit. The mass of humanity seemed to be rushing around, frantically trying to achieve many things at once. A dark blanket enveloped the cities – like impenetrable fog. It felt sticky, dirty, black and unhealthy. Often it was difficult to see the sky and in some larger cities people led their lives never seeing the stars at night or the blue sky during the day. What had humans done to their environment they wondered?

Team X were dismayed and horrified at the destruction of Gaia's resources. They saw that huge areas of land had been cleared of all natural vegetation, that the soil had eroded and any still left was without life. They saw huge forests destroyed by human's efforts and saw thick, dirty, smelly fumes from transport vehicles belching forth into the atmosphere. Many people were ill. How could humans do this to such a beautiful planet, Team X questioned. What had motivated them to act so?

At first they were too overwhelmed by what they saw to be able to communicate a dispassionate report, so they used their first few weeks to observe and integrate all that was taking place on Earth.

It seemed so alien to them that the tremendous amount of food that was produced so lovingly by Gaia was not distributed equally. They found there were millions of people starving in poorer countries whilst those in rich countries threw away mountains of food every day. Waste and rubbish were major problems in some areas, yet the food wastage could amply feed those people who were dying from hunger.

The greatest problem that they could see was human's thoughtforms. There was so much stinking thinking taking place that the mass of dark thoughtforms grew and grew to such enormous proportions creating monsters that were self-perpetuating. Team X could see that not only were the skies polluted and the land devastated and barren but the seas and rivers were also polluted. Humans had created a dark, dirty, unhygienic home for themselves and their children.

Team X passed on their findings to the Galactic Federation as they had quickly learned to be objective. They felt such compassion for Gaia and sent her much needed love and light daily. She welcomed their attention and their love and acknowledged their efforts.

The team observed many countries at war with each other, seemingly fighting over religious and political beliefs. It seemed as if so many humans were rigid and closed minded and adhered to those doctrines that had been passed down to them through the ages. They learned to understand the term 'one-eyed' and it seemed appropriately named.

Team X found some small pockets of loving, open and responsible people who loved and cared for the land and who expressed their gratitude for all Mother Earth's abundance. These people lived in relative peace although the civilised ways of the majority were infiltrating their long established lifestyles. The team spent some time with these groups encouraging them to re-establish ancient, spiritual rituals whereby they honoured Gaia and the Prime Creative Force, sending their collective heartfelt love and appreciation out to the ethers, explaining that this energy of love is such a potent force for good. They encouraged the tribes to live in harmony and explained to them the situation that existed in the 'civilised' world. The tribes were not afraid when Team X appeared in their third dimensional reality as they had experienced their visitations in earlier dream states and were prepared. Team X had been careful not to frighten or alarm the indigenous people. These people were more open minded than civilised humans and had the mental intuitive and psychic capabilities to see and feel the visitors' pure intentions.

The visitors explained how the minds of most humans living on Earth were being manipulated by the dark forces and how humans had a free will choice to allow themselves to be controlled or not. They talked to the tribes about etheric energy and how conscious understanding and application can transform energy. Team X painted a very disturbing picture of Gaia's plight to the tribes who understood and felt great empathy towards her. The tribal people vowed they would not allow themselves to be manipulated by power-hungry, greedy men. They offered to contact all their younger members who had been lured to the cities to advise them of Gaia's plight and to allow them to make up their own minds as to which path they would take. Team X recommended the tribes continue to live self-sufficient lives and to rely on their intuition and their feelings to guide them in their daily activities. Team X assisted the indigenous people to maintain peace and harmony within themselves, their families and the land. They told of Gaia's restlessness and anger and how she needed to release her feelings from time to time and how this might be devastating to some. However, if they remained in loving and calm states they would fare well.

The team encouraged the tribal people to tune into higher frequencies explaining there were now so many beings from other dimensions anxious to assist both humans and Gaia but they needed to be asked. The indigenous people could feel the changes that were occurring and knew that the time was near when Gaia would move from one state of being to another. They understood they could also ascend into a higher dimensional frequency with her. They were pleased to have the support of the Galactic team and thanked them for their timely appearance.

Now it was time for the team to tackle the big job – to find people in the cities who were being awakened to the bigger perspective of life and who were now consciously choosing to open their hearts and minds to love. The team needed to develop a systematic approach and decided to start in those areas where people had greater freedom of speech and greater freedom to study diverse subjects. Team X selected some specific countries in the world where they could see the light of conscious understanding was ready to open and expand so they chose to work in these countries first. The countries, Australia, North America, Canada and Brazil had many people from different cultures and traditions living in relative harmony and peace and so there was a blending of much diverse energy.

These countries were birthing the new consciousness movement. However, the individuals who were to be the light workers in these areas needed to clear their own negativity and karma before their gifts and talents could be utilised for the greater good of the whole.

Team X continued with their spiritual rituals, also sending their collective light and love energy to Gaia daily. They focussed as well on the darker, heavier masses of thoughtforms hovering in the etheric, bombarding them with light. The great dark mass of collective thought energy hovers over those areas where people individually and collectively sent out negativity via their thoughts and emotions in the form of fears, limitations, doubts, shame, guilt, anxiety, hatred, resentment, revenge, etc. Anything and everything that is not love collects and masses together. Like attracts like.

Team X could see how the Luciferic consciousness had so much food now. Humans were not selective or discriminating as to what they chose to think – they mostly allowed their minds to be filled with darkness, negativity and ignorance. It was sad to see such a race of puppets being so easily manipulated.

The team chose to work from the etheric for this next part of their mission. They worked to impact the minds of those humans who had asked for guidance and aid and who were consciously working with the light. Team X adhered to universal law whereby all on Earth have free will to choose their life direction. They would not break this law, as they knew that to do so would incur dark karma for themselves.

They were able to gently awaken the open-minded humans to a higher conscious understanding of themselves and what was really taking place around them, by guiding them to specific books and classes that would unveil some of the mysteries to them. They guided these humans during meditational and dreaming times, planting the seeds of love and light. They introduced new ideas and concepts and new people for them to meet. All this was done in order to accelerate the humans' spiritual growth process.

They encouraged some to write, to paint and create music, all in order to touch others with a loving vibration in such a way as to raise consciousness. The team knew that great change can only occur through individuals and that those individuals who were able to open their hearts to feelings of love and service to humanity were those who would be the leaders of the new light brigade.

Team X focussed especially on the original Galactic volunteers who needed to awaken to conscious understanding of their heritage and to shed the cloak of darkness generated by their multitudinous incarnations upon Earth. These Galactic volunteers now needed to come into an understanding and acceptance of who they really were. Some of these original Galactic volunteers had allowed the density of their physical lives to burden them and veil them in misery and unhappiness. Some had built up huge karmic debts through lives of subservience and dependency. It was now time for these souls to be cleansed and healed. In order for this transformation to occur all their darkness needed to come up from their subconscious into the light of conscious understanding. The time was fast approaching when they would be needed to play leadership roles and shine their light to the masses.

Team X guided these light workers in their self-discovery process – enabling the star seeds to open the veils of consciousness through much depth clearing of learned egotistical behavioural traits. There was much psychological baggage to clear in a relatively short period of time if they were to play the roles they had volunteered so long ago to play. As soon as the original Galactic volunteers had begun to be awakened they were introduced to new concepts and the people would could assist them in opening their hearts and minds to the bigger picture of their existence. They were encouraged to remember their origins. Once they learned to ask for help from the higher realms and to see from a bigger and wider perspective, their lives started accelerating. They drew to them events and people who could assist with their evolutionary process.

The Spiritual Hierarchy and the ET alliances were also impulsing the volunteer star seeds showing them the way through inner guidance. These interdimensional beings work on the inner planes of human awareness and consciousness. In humans' quiet and meditative moments they were able to sow the seeds of love and wisdom. Through their collective efforts they were able to awaken many human beings to a more conscious understanding of themselves and their place in the universe. They were doing this in many ways, one of them by impulsing many to become aware and more conscious of themselves through the aid of the great cosmic tool – astrology.

Many humans were also beginning to understand that matter and spirit were the same, simply vibrating at different frequencies and that all is energy and all is connected to the Divine Source.

Team X continued to work with the star seeds, encouraging the individuals to form groups. This way combined energies could mix and blend and harmonious and loving thoughtforms could be generated. Many volunteer star seeds were guided to remember ancient healing techniques, ones they had practiced in the Lemurian and Atlantean times.

The use of crystal energy began to become more widespread as people discovered how much lighter and calmer they felt after crystal healing treatments. Crystals were also being used extensively in communication technology and this was becoming a huge industry. New techniques were being discovered and new ways of communicating globally were trialed.

Team X decided it was time to call for more help. They observed how much darkness was on the planet and reported on all they observed. They believed those light workers who were awakening to their spiritual identities needed extra help. They proposed to the Galactic Federation that three more teams come to assist them, each team working one of the four countries. They recommended this be done at a particularly auspicious time when the planets in the solar system were in certain alignments.

The Galactic Federation sought more volunteers to form three more teams and these then descended into the third dimensional energy system. The light work could now expand and grow even more. The teams still had to observe and record their findings, as well as to bring more light and love into the hearts and minds of humans.

The material world was very dense and heavy and the team members had to be on guard consciously at all times. They had to be aware when they felt their energy draining from them. It was easy in their home terrain to keep their precious life force energy at its maximum peak but here on Earth constant vigilance was needed. It was apparent to them how humans readily gave their energy away to others, mostly unconsciously, and how this debilitated and drained them. They also saw how humans stole energy from others by their aggressive and self-centred behavioural traits. Both were an abuse of life force energy.

The teams continued to work quietly from the etheric planes, encouraging, inspiring, enthusing people to learn and study the higher sciences, those ancient subjects such as astrology and metaphysics, which help bring awareness and higher consciousness. They loved it when they could see their students open up to higher and broader concepts.

They encouraged people to learn spiritual practices, especially meditation, as this enabled the practitioners to open up their energy centres to new, more refined energy when their minds and bodies were calm and centred. Once they had awakened individuals they then encouraged that individual to ask for personal guidance from the higher realms and to learn to trust their intuition, their bodily sensations and their feeling nature. Having felt that the individual had advanced to this level they moved on to begin the process with another.

Gradually a bevy of light workers was being born. Many individuals all over the planet were opening up to spiritual understanding. They were opening their hearts and minds and were willing to confront and move through their own karmic residue and past life patterning. This took great courage and persistence but they were willing to confront their own self-imposed internal dragons and to take responsibility for their lives and their spiritual mission. Mostly the light workers were unclear as to where their journey would take them, however, they felt compelled to take it. As they became more aware and conscious of themselves the more their energy field expanded and the more higher knowledge they could integrate.

Up to this point in time most humans were only using a small part of their brain capacity and were stuck in their left brain linear ideas and understandings. Through meditation and creative pursuits the right hemisphere of their brain opened and expanded resulting in the capacity to integrate broader perspectives and higher knowledge

All the teams observed, recorded and reported the status on Earth. Gaia could feel more light upon her and was so grateful.

10. THE LIGHT ACCELERATES

By this time the teams working with love and light were succeeding in opening many light workers to a higher conscious understanding of themselves and the universe. Many were now able to open their hearts to the higher vibration of love. They were beginning to feel lighter, happier and more fulfilled in their daily lives. Appreciating nature and all that Mother Earth provided, they could feel love and compassion for their fellow creatures, both human and animal.

Of course, there was much karma for them to clear and this is always accelerated when one commits to the path of light and love. People can go through periods of very deep emotional lows and highs until such time as the dense dark emotional energy that has been stored in their cellular memory banks for aeons is consciously released and a new way of acting and being takes form.

The path is not always easy and it takes great courage to face one's own inner dragons and get to the source of them. Some humans imagine that they can attain a state of bliss and enlightenment without doing the inner work, however, this cannot happen. Dark energy needs to be transformed into light. Thought and emotion are energy.

The teams were diligently working at their own pace to open up the hearts and minds of humans to higher understanding and awareness. More and more people were becoming conscious of themselves in action.

The original volunteers, the star seeds, were awakening very quickly and remembering their origins. They now found it relatively easy to tap into their prior lives to see what self destructive patterns from their past were restricting them in their current lives. Those wise ones were eager to act to change their mind programmes consciously once they could see the cause of it and the effect it was having in their current life.

Often though, humans accessed their past lives and simply observed their negative patterning and chose not act differently to change those past ways of being. They didn't want to take responsibility for what they had created in previous lives and chose to remain stuck in that energy in their current life. We can understand that and make no judgement. We know it is difficult to live in the third dimensional energies. There is so much fear.

We do encourage people to choose consciously to live their lives in a more balanced and loving state by taking action to remove all that is not loving from their inner nature. This requires one to act lovingly, to think lovingly and to feel loving.

The teams were working towards the more densely populated areas by now. They had encouraged those in the less populated areas to write, paint and create music that was inspirational, uplifting and loving. These works of art were now being sought out by those in the more densely populated cities. It was like manna from heaven to them. It was something to appease their spiritual hunger and thirst. The books and magazines were devoured by the inhabitants of the major cities and more awakenings occurred. Many New Age stores began to open.

Many new world teachers were emerging, spreading light and love wherever they travelled. They were in demand and they drew people to them like a magnet. Their energy fields were now magnetic as they were vibrating to a higher frequency, the frequency of love. Their words, concepts and wisdom were being guided by us or other light beings serving with love.

The light movement was gathering force.

11. COVERT MANIPULATION

The dark forces continued to covertly impose their views, their doctrines and their power over others. People in general were unaware of the ways in which they were being manipulated. They chose to remain in ignorance rather than see the light and to be it.

Those who were becoming conscious of their spiritual selves and who were aware of how the forces of darkness operate were quietly working in their own way to spread more light. Many fine healers, astrologers, mystics, psychics and philosophers were being birthed and the movement was growing. The cosmic alignments were taking shape and many geometric patterns were being woven in the skies.

There were some harbingers of change in the form of comets that entered the solar system for a specific purpose. Their role was to bring awareness and higher consciousness to humans on Earth. They came into Earths' field to send energy to Gaia and to all living things upon her. Many humans were opened spiritually by these maverick cosmic bodies and some humans were able to tune in to their messages. Those that sent these great bodies of energy were pleased with the effect they had on humans' minds and hearts. A mass awakening was taking place.

The Galactic Federation and all their myriads of

servers were working consciously and diligently to aid Gaia and the humans upon her to raise their consciousness level – to raise their frequency. Crop circles began appearing all over the lands. These also contained symbolic formations of energy and were coded to awaken humans to a broader understanding of their spiritual heritage. Pictures of the crop circles stirred memories in humans' psyche, of times gone by.

The beings from other places in space were doing their bit to open humans to higher knowledge. The energy emanating from the symbolic designs also aided Gaia through energy transference.

People on Earth began to question – to open up to broader perspectives. However, the media chose to play down the phenomena. Those in power didn't want people questioning as that could lead to free thinking. That certainly was not on their planned agenda.

Movies were made about extra-terrestial intelligence. Most of the movies depicted the ET's to be bad guys, into power and control games and these movies were aimed to fill human hearts and minds with fear. A great tactic to render humans powerless. An occasional movie portrayed ET's as coming from a place of love and light yet these movies often did not receive the funding they needed to distribute them widely to the public. The power brokers made sure of that.

Many people were experiencing difficulties in finding work, especially meaningful work and, as they were given hand outs from the various governments which met their every day needs, they developed an indolent, lazy way of life. Many people lived their lives without any sense of meaning and purpose. They felt empty, dull, bored, frustrated and unfulfilled. Often, through peer pressure or boredom, they turned to drugs, prostitution and alcohol for their kicks. They gave away their power and their will and became even greater pawns in the dark net.

Bigger companies began devouring small companies. Small companies and businesses began to find it increasingly difficult to manage on their meagre profits. Many small businesses closed due to their inability to compete with larger businesses. The big giants were devouring the small players. More and more people were declaring bankruptcy and more and more people were committing suicide.

The young people, especially the men, were killing themselves because of a lack of purpose and meaning in their lives. They looked around their world and found it stultifying, cold, impersonal, unloving and they felt so alienated, depressed and alone. They didn't want to live in such a cold, uncaring, unhealthy planet any more. As they could see no future for themselves, they opted out. On some level of their being they knew they would have to reincarnate again, probably very quickly and take over from where they left off. This is the case with all souls. Karmic debts must be paid, evolution will occur. How long this takes is up to each individual soul.

The power brokers were playing with more germ warfare and were experimenting with other insidious viruses that could easily decimate millions, should they be released. The power brokers were biding their time. It was an ace they were holding should the light become too strong. They were also experimenting with genetics and were now able to make clones just as they did in Atlantean times. Their experiments were often carried out in deep underground buildings. They were also experimenting with abominable genetic mixes – just for fun – again like Atlantean times. Power had gone to their heads.

Many humans in so called high places were working in secret with dark ET forces, often in underground buildings mostly in remote areas of sparsely populated lands, such as Australia – to create all sorts of advanced technology. Many experiments were trialed but never were permitted to reach the minds of the general public. All these clandestine activities were accomplished far away from prying eyes. The power moguls kept a tight reign on their power tools.

Some of the churches were incredibly wealthy and had been for centuries. The power brokers loved the way people would give their money to the churches so that they could be saved from descent into 'hell' after death. The dark forces chuckled at the gullibility of the masses that had been fed these stories for two thousand years. The church systems were preying on the fear of the people and had placed the fear there in the beginning.

Many new religions were being offered to spiritually hungry humans. Some of these religions were also grubbing for control over the collective by their propaganda techniques and their ability to sway the masses. These religions also became very rich, very quickly.

There were some religions springing up that didn't want to take control of human minds and were not into extracting money from people. These religions were more interested in opening people's hearts and minds to love and light and to help bring people to a higher conscious and more aware state. These were few.

Wars continued to break out all around the globe as people continued to hold onto ancient religious beliefs and attitudes. Millions were killed every year – all in the name of God.

Jesus' teachings of love, wisdom and truth lay smouldering underneath the raging fires of hate, power, control and revenge.

Humankind was approaching an abyss.

12. THE BATTLE GROUND ESTABLISHED

The Earth was becoming more and more polluted as more humans dumped their waste and garbage upon her. Rubbish was accumulating all over the planet. A great deal of this garbage was made from material that couldn't disintegrate. Gaia could not absorb all the poisonous toxins and they made her feel very ill. Her restlessness grew. Humans were producing nuclear waste that was being stored in containers they believed would last indefinitely. 'How could humans be so ignorant'? thought Gaia. 'When I have to release the negativity dumped upon me, the containers will split asunder.'

Gaia had to stay focussed on her path. It was not her concern that the humans upon her acted so strangely and so destructively. All she could do was give out uncondi- tional love to all and keep on producing abundance. When the time was right she would cleanse herself of the negativity upon her.

She felt saddened because humans couldn't see this.

Gaia was so grateful to the Galactic Federation for responding to her call for help. She could feel herself becoming cleaner and lighter in those areas where the original volunteers and the Galactic teams were working for her. The more light and love she felt the more darkness would be transformed and the less need she would have to expel negative energy from her field. She could feel the effect of the light workers and this was gratifying to her.

There were many humans who were now consciously working on recharging her energy grid lines by specific energetic healing processes. Wherever humans had taken great quantities of precious metals and stones from her belly, great imbalances had occurred and some sensitive humans were able to do their bit to restore some of these imbalances. These were humans who tuned into her energy field, her ley lines, and were able to do spiritual rituals, tone and place power crystals upon these points. This loving energy helped bring balance to Gaia's grid system. The ancient stone circles and standing stones also helped to keep her energy field harmonised.

Gaia had been raped badly and was hurting. She was willing to give some of her vital resources to humans when there was great need or when they couldn't substitute her precious metals and gems for anything else, but her abundance had been abused. Greed had taken over the minds of men and they wanted her resources to make money for themselves, not because it was for the greater good of humankind. She couldn't understand why they abused her so and why they used fossil fuel to pollute her atmosphere when there was so much natural, clean energy so readily available.

The indigenous people of many lands understood Gaia and they were doing their best to protect her well-being by blocking any further abuse of her precious minerals. They feel her pain and appreciate her position. They love her as their mother.

Gaia could sense the time was fast approaching for a

further release of the negativity upon her. She carefully watched the movements of the planets in the solar system moving through the zodiacal signs and knew the energies emanating from them were gathering force to bring about change. She could feel the photon energy as she moved into the band and knew it would accelerate her process as well as those humans upon her. She knew more shaking up was to occur.

She could sense a build up of new energy being beamed to her from the spiritual dimensions as well. She knew she had much support.

Momentum was gathering. A new spiritual renaissance was occurring. People were awakening to the understanding that they were not just a physical body but were, in fact, spirit and that their spirit, in the form of consciousness, goes on forever. Gaia could feel the excitement as this concept dawned in the hearts and minds of humans. It was time for them to move into the light of conscious understanding and to let go of the dogma and indoctrination of the ages. Gaia was not quite so troubled now. She could see the number of light workers was growing quickly and she could feel the affect of this upon her energy field.

The Luciferic consciousness could also see that its blanket of dark was being penetrated by light. However, it had become quite complacent, as it had so much food and so much fun. It didn't really worry at all when the little pockets of light upon Earth began to grow. It was so used to abusing power by control and manipulative methods that it thought the light workers' technique of love and openness quite childish and ridiculous. In fact, it felt embarrassed by the technique. Their puppets, the power brokers, could see the light movement gathering strength and also laughed derisively at what they perceived to be puny attempts to bring about change to human nature.

They knew money and power were everything and that was all that mattered in their material world and they had more money and more power than anyone else on Earth so they would always be in charge. They believed their control was absolute and nothing could penetrate their net. They had control of the masses' minds via their educational and communication systems, control of their bodies via the drug and medical systems and control of their spiritual well-being through the churches. What else was there? They continued their games and played their puppets like pawns, taking more and more control over them as they accessed their weaknesses and used their findings for blackmail. Money was their god. Greed was their creed. Power was their goal.

Team X reported to the Galactic Federation all they observed of the dark forces also. That was their mission and they were determined to carry it out. Even though it appeared to them that the balance between dark and light was still favouring the dark, they could see that with time a definite swing to the field of light would take place. This knowledge accelerated their desire to assist those willing to commit to working with the light and opening up their understanding and perspectives.

What was happening on Earth at this particular time of her evolutionary journey was a war between the dark and light forces. What was being demonstrated by the masses was also being felt internally by each individual. The prophesised battle between opposing forces was taking place. It was very visible for those who chose to see it. Most people, however, were too engrossed in their daily lives to take the time out to view the higher perspective. In the western world people would race through their day, doing what they believed they had to do, based on their programming, then race home to eat and sit stupified in front of the television whilst the power brokers fed them trivia and lies.

The awakening souls began to slow down their lives, take time out to be in nature, spend time reading material that would raise their consciousness and learned to still their mind by meditational and contemplative practices. They began to appreciate their lives and to understand they were incarnate for a reason and purpose. They began to appreciate Gaia and all she provided and expressed their gratitude by caring for her.

The battle ground was established.

However, while the players were hooked into their own games there was still time for the players to change sides.

13. NOW IS CHOICE TIME

At this critical time in Gaia's life many changes are taking place within and without her. It is a time of monumental change as never before seen in her history. It is the time for her to ascend to a higher frequency range, to move into another dimension. She will do this. It is according to the Divine Plan.

In order to do this she needs to cleanse herself of all negativity and darkness accumulated by her over her long lifetime. She intends to become the pure, pristine, clear being that she was created to be. She will not tolerate abuse to her body for much longer.

She understands that humans are being offered another chance to move into light – to travel with her to a higher vibration. She is pleased to welcome all who love, honour and respect her. She is not greedy and gives out her love and abundance to all.

Gaia is completing a 320 million year cycle and moving into a higher spiral of evolution. At the same time she is moving into the photon band – a band of higher vibrational, fine light energy and will remain in this photon band for approximately two thousand years. She is also processing into a new age – the Age of Aquarius. All these cycles are occurring simultaneously. This has never occurred before in her history. It is a most auspicious time.

Another planet has been prepared to take her place in the third dimension. A second Earth. All those who choose to remain unconscious and stuck in their dense matter will re-incarnate upon that place and will continue with their process much the same as they have experienced for the past 26,000 years. There will be little change for them and no raising of consciousness. That is their choice and we honour it.

Those who consciously choose to work on clearing their density and darkness that take the form of fears, doubts, limitations, powerlessness, control, manipulation, greed, judgments, shame, guilt etc. and who place their strong intention and their commitment, to serve their fellow man through love and light, will ascend to the fifth dimensional plane with Gaia. There are many beings who exist on the fifth dimensional plane and beyond and they are willing to assist as this great evolutionary leap takes place. Many are working now from their own dimensions to aid individuals on Earth whenever they can achieve access and have been asked.

We, the Arcturians, wish to make the position abundantly clear to all humans so that you can exercise your free will choice to ascend with Gaia or remain in the denseness of third dimensional activity.

It is interesting for us to note that what is happening on Earth today is like a great re-play of that which happened during Atlantean times. Many of those souls who incarnated during the heyday of Atlantis are now playing out in their current incarnation of the roles they played then. Will the same fate befall nations on Earth as happened then?

Humans, you create your own fate – your own reality – through the choices you make.

Gaia has made her choice.

What do you choose?

Part Three

1. HEALING KARMIC RESIDUE

We, the Arcturians have come to assist people on Earth raise their level of consciousness to a higher plane. We come with love in our hearts. Our desire is not to manipulate or control. We respect and honour your free will to choose your path. We see our role as that of a messenger – working through willing humans to bring our truths. Please understand we have our own perspective as each of you have your own perspectives. If this material feels true to you in your heart then know it to be so.

We choose to awaken humans to their great and wonderful potential. We choose to do this through love. Light is information and the more information you have that feels true in your hearts the more light you will carry and the higher your frequency will rise.

We, the Arcturians, have come to you at this time to prepare you for that which is to come. We do what we can in our capacity as servers. However, we do need to be asked for assistance, as does any spiritual being who comes from a place of love and light. We will not abuse your free will.

We now offer some techniques which you can use to aid you in your evolutionary journey. We pass these on to you in the hope that you will integrate them into your daily lives.

As you have seen in the story, there is a crisis upon Earth, a time when the dark forces have control of the minds of humans. You have also seen how there is an acceleration of light workers lovingly serving their fellow humans through teaching, healing and writing. One of the things you can do for yourselves to raise your frequency, your vibration, your level of conscious understanding of yourself and your world, is to attend classes that are given by purely loving beings. These humans will not charge high rates for their work – they will not be high profile people, into extensive self promoting and they will live simple and meaningful lives with their prime motivation being that of service to humanity and Gaia.

More and more books will be coming out, having been written by these beings of light and love and these books will catch your eye and call your heart. Allow your heart to feel when choosing your reading matter. If you feel your heart leap with joy and excitement when you are drawn to a book, know that book is there for you to read and to learn. Your soul will be urging you to follow your heart's joy.

The same applies to any classes you attend. When you feel drawn to a particular learning environment, feel into your heart and question whether it is joyful and alive or whether it feels deadened. If joyful and excited then know that form of teaching is for you.

Your mind programme will try and manipulate you to follow your 'shoulds'. I 'should' read this or I 'should' attend this class. Learn to recognise your 'should' programmes and know they are coming from your ego, your conditioned mind, and are not coming from a place of love and spiritual advancement.

It is important also to be aware of gurus who insist their way is the only way and urge, demand, that you follow their teachings. These people are coming from a place of control and domination and from a giant ego trip. That is their way. You can choose to be discriminating and discerning and move away. Often these people find you when you are down, depressed and weakened in spirit and they latch onto you like a leech and you give all your power, your energy, away to them because you think they will rescue you from your self-imposed weakness. These people may temporarily give you solace, however, they will suck you dry if they can. They want more converts to their doctrines and more money for their coffers and this is how they feel more powerful. Be discerning of your body, your heart. Feel if there is love and joy coming from these people or whether they simply use words to manipulate.

You are in charge of your own lives and as such create whatever reality you choose to manifest for yourselves. You do this by your thoughts. We now offer another technique to assist you in creating a more loving and fulfilled life. Become acutely aware of your thoughts. Focus on what you think and what you say. When your thoughts are loving and uplifting your body will be in harmony. Whenever your body is out of ease it will be because of negative and self-sabotaging thoughts. Be aware and tune into your self.

Thoughts and words have energy. Whenever a thought, in the form of energy, goes out into the ethers it attracts the same kind of energy to itself in the form of situations and experiences. This is how the universal law of 'like attracts like' works. It is the law of attraction. You will attract to you that which you are thinking and feeling. The energy of the universe is very magnanimous. It will give back to you that which you are thinking and feeling. It is so important, therefore, to become conscious of the thoughts you think and the emotions you feel.

As an example – If you continue to want and feel lack, in any area of your life, this is what you will draw to yourself – e.g., more wanting and more lack. This is how energy works. Like attracts like.

In order to feel abundant, joyful and loving, you need to think loving, joyful and abundant thoughts about yourself and your life at all times. It will take much conscious awareness and focusing on your own mind programmes. However, this is what is needed in order for changes to occur for you. Should you be willing to commit to a loving and ligh- filled life you will need to act consciously to bring about the changes inside of yourself. As you then consciously change to become more light- filled people around you will notice this and feel your love. You will then begin to attract more loving people, events and circumstances into your life that fill you with joy. It really is that simple.

We now come to another step you can take in order to bring yourselves into a more enlightened state and that is to learn to take personal responsibility for all you have created in your world.

Your thoughts create your experiences in your life and you need to accept total responsibility for this.

The law of karma is in effect here. That which you create, through your thoughts and actions, will always come to you. For example, if you played out, in some past life, the game of power and control over others, then this lifetime you will need to experience how it feels to be powerless. The issue is one of power and the abuse of that energy. Both polarities of the energy need to be experienced before balance can exist. Once you have consciously recognised the issue and are clear about how it has been played out in your life, or lives, then you can call a halt to the imbalance, consciously. You can choose to no longer play the game of either powerless, or power over, and simply choose to come into your own power through your heart via love. You can make the change instantly. Of course, it takes effort, will, discipline and acute awareness of self in action. However, your external world is a wonderful mirror for where you are at in your lives.

You may not understand what we mean by playing power over, or playing powerless in your lives. Let us use an example. Many women allow their partners or husbands to have a dominating, controlling and powerful influence over them and give their power away to their men. This giving away of power or energy depletes them and in time illness will occur. The male will continue to play the power over game because the woman allows him to. Both parties are operating from darkness, rather than from love and the light of understanding. It is up to the individuals involved to understand this power game and to change the dynamics once conscious awareness of the game is understood.

Let us illustrate another power issue.

Should you have been sexually abused in your childhood, and this is a very real, dark issue for humankind at this time, know that at sometime in your past lives you played out the game of sexual abuser. Once you can view the incident from this higher perspective, the emotional charge you have associated with the incident dissipates because you have accepted that only you are responsible. You would know that you had only drawn the abuse to you because you carried that dark energy inside of you, albeit unconsciously. Light is conscious understanding.

This brings us to another powerful technique for recognising the darkness within – the mirror technique. If your life is not working for you in any area, for instance, should you be lacking in material abundance, then that lack of material abundance in your external world is simply mirroring back to you, via a reflection, the lack you think and feel in your inner world. You may be unconsciously sabotaging by thinking you are undeserving of abundance, unworthy of having abundance, or think poverty is best suited to spiritual people – whatever – there are a myriad of self-defeating thoughts that can create lack of abundance in one's life. You are the one creating your world through your thoughts.

You will continue to attract into your life exactly what it is you put out. It is therefore important to recognise that only you are totally responsible for your life and what is happening in it. You have created it that way – albeit unconsciously. Accepting personal responsibility for everything you create in your life, everything, raises your frequency level considerably and brings about more lightness of being. Whenever there is acceptance of responsibility there is no blame. Whenever one blames another person, thing, or incident in their lives for the state they find themselves in, then know that one is not taking personal responsibility for themselves.

For example, should you feel, angry, upset, hurt, or betrayed when another triggers you into emotional re-action, know that person is simply your teacher, showing you that you still have darkness inside of you in the form of those emotional reactions. When you choose to see the person in this light, you can be grateful and acknowledge that there is still more karma for you to clear from your psyche. This is taking personal responsibility for your own state of being.

When one focuses on one's own energy patterns and is willing to accept responsibility for all one has created, then doors open on all levels of existence. The evolution of the soul is what is important here so it doesn't matter how long or how many lifetimes this karma takes. Balance is what the soul requires, and a clearing of the karmic debt.

Be aware people. If you feel frustrated, for instance, when sitting in a traffic jam and veer off, impulsively, on another route, the energy of frustration is likely to create more frustration– what you put out, you get back. On the other hand should you sit calmly and quietly in the traffic jam and accept that this is how it is and that there may be a reason for this – one that you cannot see from your limited perspective – then you will be putting out the energy of patience and calm and that is what you will receive.

When you are willing to take personal responsibility for all you have created in your life and accept objectively your situation and have let go of any emotional charge around issues in your life then the energy changes – transmutes – and the karma is over. Balance reigns.

At this time in Gaia's history there is much karma being played out, much of it unfinished business from past lifetimes that is being brought into conscious awareness. It is time for karma to be cleared, consciously. You have been collecting dark thoughts and feelings for the past 26,000 years and now, as the Age of Light, the Age of Aquarius is upon you it is time to deal with your accumulated karma once and for all. You can call a stop to your dysfunctional games, now.

We, and many other light beings, are here to help you. However, you need to ask for our help. We will not impose our will upon you. We cannot deal with your karma for you, it is not our responsibility. However, we can assist by bringing to you situations and people into your life who will help you with the process. You need to become aware of this and always look for the deeper meanings. As humans move into the Age of Light, the age of higher consciousness, with Gaia, you will become more conscious of yourself in word, deed and thought. This is what evolution is all about – to become lighter, more consciously aware human beings.

We offer yet another technique for bringing you into a higher state of conscious understanding of yourselves, a higher degree of light, and that is to bring to your awareness the concept of time.

Earth time is different to that of other planets and

galaxies. Time on Earth has been fabricated to fit into a man-made structure of a calendar. This calendar does not correspond to any celestial phenomena. It was devised purely on the whim of a power- hungry male and then altered by one of the Roman Catholic faith many centuries later.

People on Earth, you have hooked yourselves into a structure and attempted to fit into an unnatural system. In other energetic bodies in the cosmos, time is more elastic and beings who live in other systems live much, much longer than Earthlings because they are not geared into any rigid structure.

We ask you to become aware of yourselves and how you allow 'time' to rule you. Are you a clock watcher, checking always – perhaps even a hundred times a day, to see whether you have 'time' for this and that? Be aware that you are being regulated by a system that is totally artificial.

Allowing yourselves to flow with the rhythms of nature, the currents of energy that flow through you, is life enhancing. Forcing yourselves to adhere to rigid time structures is life destroying. Learning to tune into your bodies, to sense and feel what you body is needing will help you become more aware of your own cycles and rhythms. Sometimes your body may feel like exp-eriencing exercise and sometimes it might feel like being quiet and still. Tune in and allow yourself flexibility in your daily lives. When you go with the flow of your energy patterns you will feel more alive, more alert and better able to deal with your daily activities. This leads to better health. Be aware of your time commitments and give yourself flexibility to meet these commitments. Allow the energy to flow – allow the light of understanding to shine from you.

Another important factor to bring to conscious awareness is to question yourselves as to how much time you spend each day dwelling in the past. "Oh, I should have said such and such to that person in my conversation yesterday," or "I am angry and upset by what happened three weeks ago and I can't get it out of my mind," or "My parents believed such and such to be true and so I act out their beliefs and wonder why I'm stuck in my life."

The past is over, it cannot be changed and the future never comes, so why waste your precious energy by thinking about it.

What you think, feel and do in your present time is what creates your future, so if you think, feel and do light and loving things then your future will be loving and light.

Tune in to the moment – live joyously in that moment. Feel your spirit in that moment. Become aware of yourself in this present moment – are you feeling dark, depressed, sad, unmotivated, weak or are you feeling light, bright, happy, cheerful and positive? What future are you creating for yourself?

You may choose to question yourselves as to whether you like to be in control of your future whereby you plan every action down to the last detail. It is wonderful to plan but then the plans need to be released so that spontaneity of the moment can be experienced.

Spontaneity is connected to the heart. Just think of how a little child plays. Is the child clock watching or is it allowing the universal energy to work through it?

A child's life, when parents let go of control, can be wondrously joyful. Light and love shine through the child because that child is living totally in present time. They trust their needs will be met and they trust that there is plenty of 'time' to act spontaneously and have fun. They do not have a care for the past or the future.

You, as adults, can also experience this love and joy, which is your natural state, once you let go of your attachment to being regulated by time. Many wonderful opportunities can be missed when you elect to be inflexible and rigid with your time.

The energy from the cosmos is there to serve you and aid you to be abundant, healthy and happy. All have the same amount of energy, all have the same amount of 'time'.

You can accomplish your tasks with joy, flexibility and spontaneity or you can choose to hold on to the structures that bind and bring about limitations.

As always the choice is yours.

2. THE SETTING OF INTENTION

We, the Arcturians, ask you to choose your path very carefully, to become aware of when you may stumble or go on a difficult track. Allow your outside world to be your mirror to your inside world. Should your external life reflect back to your struggle and hardship then know it is but a reflection of your inner world.

When you become aware that your outside reality is full of struggle, intend to change consciously your inner world. Your intention carries a strong vibration. If your intention to change is truly heartfelt and you focus your thought upon this intention, you will receive circumstances, events or people into your life who will help you towards fulfilling your intention.

Following the intention there needs to be a commitment to your own path to higher consciousness to light, which is your own path back to the Divine Source of All Things. This is the spiritual path and the way to internal peace, balance and harmony.

This peace, balance and harmony is a state, a feeling of bliss, of at-one-ment with all, a feeling of joy for the sake of joy and a feeling of great love and appreciation for all of creation. This state is unity with All That Is. This is where the state of higher consciousness leads. It needs a commitment and an intention, both heartfelt, to reach this place. It requires awareness of one's thoughts, emotions and actions. It means learning to be objective and impersonal and to see the larger perspective of life. All this takes practice.

It will not automatically occur because you wish it to. You are the ones who are responsible for your states of being. You make your choices as to the state you are in. We honour your choices. We are simply offering you some tools to accelerate your process, enabling you to become a more enlightened human being – a being of higher frequency – should you choose to act upon them.

Choosing to act upon these guidelines you then know that not only will you be aiding yourselves but you will be aiding all those in your sphere of influence. You will also be aiding Gaia as you will be bringing into your being a higher vibration of a more refined energy – that of light and love – replacing the darkness and denseness that exists. You would be making a conscious choice to follow the light. This is the way to become a light worker.

We will continue and offer more tools for your higher understanding and awareness of self in thought, emotion and deed.

Once you have placed your heartfelt intention out to the ethers and have made your strong commitment to change your dark internal patterns of being, then you will find situations and people 'in your face' who are there to help accelerate your process. You need to be aware that this will happen. These situations and people are there because your higher self has called them to you, the personality self, in order that you begin to think, feel and act differently.

This is the challenge for you to change. This may bring

up self doubt, fears, feelings of unworthiness etc., however, this is your opportunity and as such needs to be embraced consciously. You will be able to see where you have restricted your flow of abundance, you will see where you have limited yourself and you will see where you have fears. These are part of your darkness and have been patterns that you have carried around for aeons of time. You can now choose to break this denseness and transmute it into lighter energy by busting through your old patterns with courage and confidence. You can choose to respond to the situations and the people rather than re-acting to them.

Your instinctive, re-actionary patterns are those that contain the darkness or absence of light. They cover up thoughts and emotions of lack, doubt, fear, insecurities, anger, hurt, sadness, and these patterns of negativity are what hold you back from evolving into a lighter state of being.

The road to the light can be easy or it can be difficult. You are the one who chooses your path. Each one has their own individual path to higher consciousness, a higher frequency of energy and you will all get there. That is part of the Divine Plan. How long it takes is up to you.

At this time in the history of humankind we offer you tools to aid your ascension process. You can consciously ascend with Gaia to that of a higher frequency and move with her into another dimension and experience great peace, joy, fulfilment, happiness and good health in your life, or you can continue to remain in your 3D unconscious games for many more incarnations. It is your choice.

Another wonderful tool we offer to you is to be discerning of your body and its messages. Your physical body is a precious and most wondrous system of intelligence. It is packed so full of wisdom and knowledge and carries in all its cells, memories of your history. It is a wondrous system of energy.

When your body is functioning well you feel alive, bright, alert, energised and at ease. Your body is registering that your thoughts and emotions are healthy and light.

When your body is out of ease, or in dis-ease, then know that it is your thoughts and emotions that are causing that disease.

For example: You may have spent much of your life thinking that you needed to please others and therefore never considered your own needs. This would then lead to many deep, dark thoughts of envy, jealousy, hatred, and possibly revenge, though these thoughts may be unconscious. The thought energy forms into dark emotions. You will feel these emotions. They represent a blockage of energy in your internal circuitry system. The light and love of understanding is blocked and is unable to move through your body freely. The dense, dark energy then gathers more to it, the more you think the dark thoughts. It forms a 'ball' of negativity, of denseness; a blockage is formed. This dark energy then begins to eat into your organs. It becomes an entity in its own right. Your thoughtforms have gathered mass and have lodged in your body. A disease then manifests, such as cancer of the bowel or the reproductive organs.

The physical body is the final destination of the dark

thoughts. They first form in the mental body, a finer subtle energy body, and then move to the emotional body and finally manifest as disease in the physical body.

Whenever you are out of ease in the physical body know that the ache, pain or irritation, contains a message for you, one that requires your attention. Your body will be communicating a message to you that you are indulging in dark thoughts and emotions and these need to be understood and addressed.

Whenever you have rashes, inflammations, boils or eruptions of the skin, know that there is some frustration and suppressed anger inside of you and is manifesting as the angry symptoms. When you, with conscious awareness and understanding, responsibly deal with your inner frustrations and anger, the symptoms will disappear. The blocked dam of energy will be released and will be transformed into light (the light of understanding and awareness) and energy will flow through your body easily.

There are many wonderful healers on this planet now who work with energy blockages and who can assist you with understanding your blockages. They can aid you. They cannot change your patterns of thought, emotion and behaviour, only you can do that by consciously becoming aware of the thoughts that do not serve you.

For example, you may unconsciously think you are not worthy of receiving love from family members, relationship partners or friends, so experience a lack of love in your life. You may think your body or face ugly, or your whole being objectionable. These are the thoughts that need to be worked with consciously if you are to receive love from your external world. Once you spend effort, time and will uncovering the source of these beliefs, and then acting to change them, at the same time believing that you are deserving of love, then your external world will begin to reflect that change. Any thoughts of unworthiness (albeit unconscious) will only bring about situations that reflect these thoughts in your life in order for you to see the truth. When a person's heart is not feeling love and joy then energetic barriers form around the heart. Over time heart problems arise.

Often a healer can tap into energetic blockages created by negative thoughts and temporarily clear them. However, until you consciously act to transform that dark energy into light your outer life cannot reflect the change.

By becoming conscious and aware of your body's messages and by changing your thoughts and emotional re-actions, you can begin to live a life that is lighter, happier, healthier and loving. This will not only aid you but all those around you, as you will be giving out more vibrant, lighter energy. If you come from a place of resentment or bitterness then this is the energy you will give out to others. Is this loving?

Open your hearts Earthlings, to the greatest energy of all. Love. Love has the highest vibration. Love is All That Is. Love is the energy all have in equal abundance. Love is the energy that promotes growth. Love is pure energy. When you consciously and daily fill yourselves with love you will feel lighter, more loving, and will radiate this energy out to others. All benefit. Gaia benefits. Through love you will ascend to a higher frequency, a higher state of being.

Love and understanding are the keys to open the door of your heart and it is through your heart that loving, warm, generous, abundant feelings flow. It is so important to learn to love yourself by honouring, respecting and accepting your own divine nature, your own uniqueness. Love of self and the understanding and sure knowledge that you are of the Divine, that you are a part of the Source of All Things, will heal your wounds, your inner darkness. Love transmutes all darkness.

Will you choose Love?

EPILOGUE

We shall now take you forward in your Earth time to that of December 2012. It is at the Northern Hemisphere winter solstice that a great shift of energy will occur.

This is the end of the Mayan calendar. By this time, humans on Earth will have made their choice, consciously or unconsciously, to ascend with Gaia to a higher frequency of light, a more aware and conscious state of being, or to stay stuck on the karmic wheel of three-dimensional life.

By this time one's spiritual body will have taken form in the etheric and the other three bodies that make up 3D reality, the physical, emotional and mental, will be relatively clear and light. Much denseness and darkness will be behind you and you will look forward to manifesting brilliant scenarios in your life. It will be a joyous and loving time. Peace will be within and peace will be without. Your energies will be more refined, you will feel more balanced and in harmony with yourselves and your lives will be fulfilling and purposeful.

You will look back on your lives with wonder and awe and find it difficult to understand how you spent so much of your life in struggle. From your new perspective it will all seem like a far distant memory – a memory showing you how blinded you were to the glories of your self, the magnificence of your self – the wonder of your self. You have all travelled a difficult road. We in distant galaxies wonder at your courage and tenacity. The three dimensional plane is one of learning about oneself through experiencing. You chose this path and some of you choose it still. For those that choose to stay enmeshed in your physical, emotional and mental constricts, you will have much time to play your games over the next 26000 years. You will continue to draw to you many experiences that may not be so pleasant in order for you to understand that only you are doing it to yourself. However long it takes is however long it takes.

Eventually, however, you too will come into higher consciousness of yourselves in thought, emotion and deed and then your light body will begin to form. You will begin to transmute your darkness into light. The dense heaviness of 3D reality will lessen and you will release your attachments to the material world.

For those of you who are at this present time undecided as to the route to take, your Higher Self will urge you to change your old stuck concepts, attitudes, beliefs about yourself and your world and this may come about through crises and trauma. If, on some higher level, you have chosen to move on to a broader and higher consciousness, then this shift in you will occur.

Humans seem to find they best move on in conscious-ness via crises. It is the most difficult route to take, however it seems to be the human way.

Gaia will ascend to a higher frequency, a higher vibratory rate, and the photon energy – that band of light – is assisting with this process. When any living thing moves into a higher frequency the internal nervous system can be affected.

Humans, you may feel great internal stress, friction, restlessness as the finer energies impact upon you. A shaking up may occur within your own energetic circuitry system. It will be so important for you to practice calming and meditative procedures to keep your mind from short circuiting.

We are here to assist you to make your transition from the 3D frequency to the 5th dimensional frequency. We are here to aid you to change your personal 'radio band' and so be able to tune into a more refined loving, light-filled life. We are here to aid your ascension into a higher conscious state of being. We do need to be asked. There are millions of other light beings all ready to also assist in your evolutionary process and we give our service willingly, lovingly and unconditionally.

Gaia may need to release the toxins and poisons from her body. She may need to shake off all the negative thoughtforms that abound upon her. She can, however, have her burden lightened by those humans who consciously, with love, effort and will, commit to clearing their own negativity, their own darkness and transform that into light, the light of conscious understanding of the dark games played. This awareness allows a higher vibration, a higher degree of light, to enter one's etheric body, however one then needs to act upon one's new awareness. It is this action that is needed in order for the transmutation of energy to occur. This takes courage, as fear can arise and this fear needs to be faced, acknowledged and then moved through consciously. If one has the awareness of negative games and continues to play them out, then much karma can accumulate. More darkness enters.

People on Earth, your lives can be so joyous, so loving, so fulfilling when you loosen your hold on your old self destructive 3D patterns of thought, emotion and behaviour.

We encourage you to develop the courage to face your own internal darkness, to place the heartfelt intention to change, to transform your negative thoughts, emotions and deeds and begin to open your hearts to feelings of love and joy. It is these feelings and these thoughts and actions that help make your light body. The more love and joy you allow yourself to feel, the more you will display this to others, the more others will feel it, bask in it, and the more life will flow harmoniously for you. All will benefit.

We trust our story strikes a cord in your heart and is a catalyst in showing you the way to a lighter, brighter, more loving life.

We now say adieu and thank our channel for the opportunity of addressing ourselves through her.

So be it.